★   ★   ★

"*The Spiritual Abraham Lincoln* is an extremely well written book that investigates what might be termed the spiritual side of President Lincoln. It's both scholarly and very readable. I came away impressed at Mr. Wyrick's portrayal of the President and with an ͨͪ˙ ˙d and enlarged vision of the man."

William Hoff̶ ͏iter; author of *Bloc͏*

"When it comes to invoking religion in support of any of their decisions, politicians need to sit at the feet of Abraham Lincoln. Reinhold Niebuhr once called him 'America's greatest theologian.' Why so great? Because he invariably distinguished between human works and the works of the Almighty. As Wyrick says, 'He wore the mantle of humility easily,' because he was more impressed with what God was doing in the world than with what he, president of the United States in the midst of an awful crisis, was doing. That is why in his last major speech he distinguished between both human causes in the Civil War and the Almighty's 'own purposes.' Lincoln would have agreed that it is better to leave God-talk out of politics than to decorate human proposals with divinity. This is a book for our American time. Through his careful study of Lincoln's career, Wyrick compels us to remember that piety belongs in politics *only* when piety transcends politics."

Dr. Donald W. Shriver
Emeritus professor at Union Theological Seminary in New York. Author of *An Ethic for Enemies: Forgiveness in Politics*

★   ★   ★

"V. Neil Wyrick's fine work allows the reader to appreciate Abraham Lincoln's Christian commitment and his prophetic role in American history. Should have a wide readership."

James H. Smylie
Professor of Church History (Ret.)
Union Theological Seminary,
Richmond, Virginia

"Neil Wyrick's *The Spiritual Abraham Lincoln* should be read by anyone attempting to understand the man who was probably the most complex person to ever hold the office of president of the United States. Dr. Wyrick is intent on demonstrating that the spirituality so often expressed in Lincoln's writings and speeches was not merely lip service to a Deity, but rather expressions of a profound faith in a real God. It was this faith that provided the wisdom, compassion, insight and sometimes steel that Lincoln would need in full measure as he led the United States through the Civil War. Dr. Wyrick's clear and unpretentious style of presentation is very much in keeping with the character of his subject, and in so doing, Wyrick makes his point very well that Lincoln, his beliefs, and the faith that formed them, are as relevant to a troubled America in 2004 as they were in 1863."

Daniel Allen Butler, author of *"Unsinkable": The Full Story of the RMS Titanic, The Lusitania* and *The Age of Cunard*

★ ★ ★ ★ ★ ★ ★ ★ ★ ★ ★

The Spiritual
Abraham
LINCOLN

★ ★ ★ ★ ★ ★ ★ ★ ★ ★ ★

The Spiritual
Abraham
LINCOLN

V. Neil Wyrick

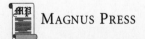 MAGNUS PRESS

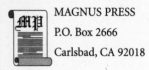

MAGNUS PRESS
P.O. Box 2666
Carlsbad, CA 92018

The Spiritual Abraham Lincoln

First Edition, 2004

Printed in the United States of America
Cover art: "President Abraham Lincoln Praying for Victory at Gettysburg, 1863" by Lloyd Ostendorf, courtesy of Rita Ostendorf and the Lincoln College Museum

LCCN: 2004103369
ISBN: 0-9724869-1-7

Publisher's Cataloging-in-Publication Data
(Prepared by The Donohue Group, Inc.)

Wyrick, V. Neil.
  The spiritual Abraham Lincoln / by V. Neil Wyrick. -- 1st ed.
  p. : ill. ; cm.
  Includes bibliographical references.
  ISBN: 0-9724869-1-7

1. Lincoln, Abraham, 1809-1865--Religion. 2. Christian life.
3. Presidents--United States--Biography. I. Title.

E457.2 .W97 2004
973.7/092 B   2004103369

---

10 09 08 07 06 05 04   10 9 8 7 6 5 4 3 2 1

To my

lovely, creative,

inspirational wife,

Tucky

FROM THE AUTHOR . . .

Someone has said that God should have made our ears twice as big and our mouths twice as small. Taking these words of wisdom to heart, I have listened enthusiastically and accepted graciously the proffered wisdom of Lincoln scholars and devotees. Countless folk have also given me treasured tidbits following my Lincoln one-man dramatizations. Besides the books listed in the bibliography, I have read numerous letters by Lincoln, to Lincoln and about Lincoln. Studying these historical documents is the closest thing to being there for an author. Often I have felt as if I were standing at a debate or striding alongside this man of distinct conscience as he moved toward his appointed destiny.

These writings have been a labor of love, and I can but hope they will help you to gain new inspiration from he who forgave so well those who would not practice the same toward him.

★　　★　　★

TABLE OF CONTENTS

PREFACE

This book is more than just a march down memory lane. It is certainly not a search-and-destroy mission as are some historical efforts. It is really a questing for an understanding of the man able to write:

"He has the right to criticize who has the heart to help."

"Am I not destroying my enemies when I make friends of them?"

"It is the duty of nations, as well as of men, to owe their dependence upon the overruling power of God. . ."[1]

"With malice toward none; with charity for all; with firmness in the right, as God gives us to see the right..."[2]

When a president continues to think and speak this way, often commenting on sin and mercy more like a preacher than a politician, it is worth scrutinizing his life. When he called out for "firmness in the right, as God gives us to see the right," he did not just show humility. Rather he asked for a national self-examination and that God might be at the center of such evaluation.

Why concern ourselves with spirituality as against the equivalent of political science? What real difference does it make that Christianity needs to be up front and center in the lives of our leaders? Because the very freedoms and style of living we enjoy come as gifts from Christianity.

Before Christ walked this earth and gave us a new standard of humanity, life in the Greco-Roman world was cheap and expendable. Killing of infants was readily accepted. Child abandonment was commonplace. Abortions and suicides were widespread and legal. Its corrupt belief system became the mother of chaos. It is, therefore, little wonder Rome fell. And America can fall just as easily if it forgets that religion can survive without freedom, but freedom cannot long survive without religion.

When ole Abe swore on the Bible to uphold the Constitution, the faith he brought with him helped him to honestly support the five references to God found in the Declaration of Independence: supreme Lawmaker, Creator, Source of certain unalienable rights, world's supreme Judge, and Protector on whom we can rely. It is not that an atheist or agnostic could not pay lip service to these, it is just that an obvious lack of enthusiasm would make its mark.

But how spiritual was Abraham Lincoln? Well, one indicator is how often he worked God into both his conversations and speeches. He was not the only president to mention prayers to the Almighty on a regular basis, but what is important is how comfortable he seemed in doing it. A single reminder of an isolated spiritual moment would make it impossible to build a case for spirituality. With Lincoln this is never a problem, for this giant of a man had an on-going sense of soul equal to his physical presence.

"I invite the people of the United States… to invoke the

influence of His Holy Spirit…"[3] It is well to remember that the man behind this national proclamation also wrote that he had a solemn oath registered in heaven to finish his work. And why not? This, after all, was a man who at Gettysburg, with generals and other men of good counsel all around, still fell to his knees in prayer, and thereby, found "sweet comfort"[4] creeping into his soul.

A secular humanist will be less than happy with these observations because it reminds us that Abraham Lincoln was a man of moral absolutes. That he knew the difference between right and wrong and agonized over them. Anyone who has a love affair with anarchy has to be unhappy with a president who did not believe that if it feels good then it must be okay.

Do you know that five hundred and fifty-five feet above the ground, there sits on top of the Washington Monument an aluminum cap upon which is etched the phrase *Laus Deo*? From this lofty height overlooking sixty-nine square miles of the District of Columbia, this Latin phrase sends out the message *Praise be to God*. On the 12th landing of its 898 monument steps, there's a prayer offered by the City of Baltimore. What of the memorial on the 20th step presented by Chinese Christians? No one argued against having Proverbs 10:7, Luke 18:16 and Proverbs 22:6 being engraved on the 24th. School children from New York and Philadelphia had suggested this and it was accepted as a splendid idea. Is there any significance that when the cornerstone was laid in 1848 a Holy Bible was put there by the Bible Society? There could, of course, have been a book on atheism or no religious book at all, but not if the leaders at that time had not truly believed that this was a "nation under God."

Our 16th president built on such cornerstones, following in the footsteps of men such as George Washington, who proclaimed in 1789, "It is the duty of all nations to acknowledge the providence of Almighty God, to obey His will, to be grateful for His benefits, and humbly to implore His protection and favor."[5] Then there was Thomas Jefferson who, before he was Chief Executive, made sure God was part of the Declaration of Independence. His request was unanimously accepted on July 4, 1776. Yet another of the Founding Fathers, still to be Commander-in-Chief, John Adams, wrote, "Statesmen may plan and speculate for liberty, but it is religion and morality alone which can establish the principles upon which freedom can securely stand."[6]

To mention Christianity and our nation in the same context today is to create a firestorm of complaint. "We must assure separation of church and state" is the politically correct outcry. Unfortunately, most who are straining their vocal chords have not strained any intellectual efforts to research how the original quote actually reads.

When Thomas Jefferson dipped his pen and began to put down his thoughts, he wrote, "a *wall* of separation between Church and State." Even more interesting is the reason why it was written. A group of less than joyous Baptists in

Connecticut did not want to have their denomination play second fiddle to the Congregationalists. The Congregationalists? They would have been perfectly willing to be top dog as the state's choice. Episcopalians in Virginia were no less reluctant to create the same problem, if given half a chance. Thomas Jefferson stuck by his guns in this state as well.

Separation of church and state? But should that mean separation of God and man?

Would it have made any difference if the man who was president of the United States during the Civil War had not been a Christian? The War took the lives of over six hundred thousand young men, one in every five of the country's best, so it is no small question to ask. Is there always the danger that a Christian leader will still be arrogant, angry and more than willing to shape pruning hooks into spears?[7] Unfortunately, yes. But not Abe. His words spell out clearly how he felt about solutions by the sword. "The man does not live who is more devoted to peace than I am. None who would do more to preserve it."[8]

No matter what he spoke, the same confusion as to who Lincoln really was existed just as much in his time as in ours. Poor fellow, wherever he spoke, almost every newspaper in the North said he had extended an olive branch and almost every paper in the South that he had extended a sword.

Lincoln was once quoted as having said, "I don't like that man. I must get to know him better." People in the South did not like that man Lincoln, and they were not about to try to get to know him better. Inexplicably both sides called out to the Prince of Peace for help in winning a war.

Into this fray a political Lincoln, a military Lincoln, and a spiritual Lincoln moved toward monumental decisions. Struggling for truth, sometimes befuddled by reality, this man who knew his Bible as well as some preachers would often be asked if he thought God was on the side of the North. His reply always remained the same. "My concern is not whether God is on our side. My great concern is to be on God's side."[9] It would be difficult to place too much emphasis on the spiritual undergirdings he brought to every decision. This child of the wilderness had had no city lights to mute the stars or compete with moonlight. He had watched his own growing, side by side with all the other growing things in field and forest. It seemed natural to him to ponder that human life must be more of mind, and soul a reality.

During the days of his youth, this gentle giant did dally with Deism, but it must also be remembered that with passing years spiritual wisdom took over. An ongoing controversy argues that he was not a Christian because he was never baptized or joined a church. It seems only fair to let his own words defend him against any who would doubt his faith. In 1846, with typical honesty he said what was and what wasn't. "That I am not a member of any Christian church is true, but I have never denied the truth of the Scriptures, and I have never spoken with intentional disrespect of religion in general, or of any denomination of Christians in particular..."

It was not that he did not believe in Christ. He said he would gladly join any church that would not overwhelm him with dogma. So, it was not a cry against Christianity, but a cry against Christians who, with determined zeal, had split up into over three hundred recognized denominations.

Though six-foot-four and weighing one hundred eighty-four pounds, Abraham Lincoln was never too big for his long-legged britches. He was not overly impressed with himself, but always impressed by the works of the Almighty.

In his growing up he knew little of the thin two hundred square mile strip of civilization hugging the eastern coast. He would, of course, live and die there one day, this man who would travel so far from the wilderness to Washington. Would travel, but never alone, for his was a soul attuned to heaven.

V. Neil Wyrick
Miami, Florida

★ ★ ★ ★ ★ ★ ★ ★ ★

Chapter 1

In the Beginning

★ ★ ★ ★ ★ ★ ★ ★ ★

One day the second child of Thomas and Nancy Hanks Lincoln would become the president of what many have called, and continue to call, the Promised Land. However, anyone voicing such a thought on the day of his birth, the twelfth of February 1809, would have been laughed at and told by any backwoods listener that he didn't have a possum's chance. Picture this future president growing up dirt poor with a shirt made of bear skins, a coonskin hat and dreams of something better than what was offered. The one-room notched log cabin in Hardin County, Kentucky certainly wasn't much of a springboard for success.

He was named after his paternal granddaddy and Abraham, in the Bible. Though the Biblical Abraham was certainly a leader, our Abe achieved leadership not because he was born to it, but because somewhere along the line he decided he would rather lead than be led.

His mother often rested the family Bible in her lap as she recited its stories to little Abe and his sister Sarah. A younger brother Thomas died at birth. With love and affection Lincoln said of her, "God bless my mother. All that I am or ever hope to be, I owe to her." He never stopped reading his Bible, which is why so many of his speeches were peppered with Scripture.

Though much of his youth was certainly an isolated existence, there was a period when their home was on the main road from Louisville to Nashville. Running right by their cabin door, it gave Lincoln the advantage of countless meetings with multi-thinking travelers. By the time the family moved again, when he was seven, he had to have listened scads of times to discussions about how government could, and needed to, improve on the shakiness of land ownership because of uncertain boundaries, high interest rates and slavery.

It was during this same time that America nearly lost its future president before they lost him to an assassination. He almost drowned in a creek. But it didn't happen. He was needed down the road for greater things.

Unfortunately, when Abe was only nine his mother died of milk fever, as did many in that time. His widowed father soon married again and if one had to have a stepmother, Lincoln could have done no better than Sally Bush. This woman, who for the rest of his life he referred to as his *angel mother*, did all she could to encourage his father to look more kindly on his love of learning. It was an exercise in futility for Tom Lincoln considered such bookish behavior a waste of time. This was how Abe came to regard his father's occupational choices.

Having two such remarkable mothers who so greatly influenced this gangling youth could almost be called providential.

The opportunity of a formal education for young Abe was close to nil. One time they lived eighteen miles from a school. That was a lot of walking between the family farm and the one room schoolhouse he called his learning home. It is one of the reasons that over his childhood he had a little less than a year's worth of actual schooling.

Because there were no books, everything was learned by rote, hence the nickname Blab Schools. Abe liked to repeat things over and over so he would never forget them, sayings such as:

"Live in your youth so you will not have to be ashamed in your old age."

"Cowards never start, the weak never finish."

"You can get more with an ounce of honey than a gallon of gall."

He tried always to live by these and other early learned schoolhouse maxims.

Nor was paper readily available. During these brief winter sessions, he would practice his lessons in the dirt or snow.

Chasing after a good book like a dog after a rabbit, he

would sometimes walk as far as twenty miles to borrow one. It was said that from the age of twelve he never went anywhere without a beloved book tucked beneath his arm. Lincoln began to develop a list of favorites: Aesop's *Fables*, thought-provoking *Pilgrim's Progress,* the works of William Shakespeare, *The Life of George Washington*, and the biographies of Ben Franklin.

One section in particular in *Pilgrim's Progress* heavily influenced his thinking. Ignorance is walking with two pilgrims and says, "My heart is as good as any man's heart…as to my thoughts, I take no notice of them."

Many of his friends chose ignorance and could neither read nor write. He was known to comment that they were not too dumb to learn, but rather too lazy. "Some," he said, "were so lazy they couldn't have raised a good stink even if they were a skunk." I can easily imagine Lincoln, with sadness for their lack of discipline, quoting Proverbs, "As he thinketh in his heart, so is he."[1]

It is one thing to know what should be done. It is always something else to do it. Surmise then that his Bible knowledge offered motivation thoughts such as "Wisdom is the principal thing; therefore get wisdom: and with all thy getting get understanding."[2]

Part of his education would today be called survival school. As in all pioneer families, the possibility of disaster was never far away. There were no guarantees when a farmer walked out his door come morning time that he would come back through that same door when dusk arrived. Abe once killed a hundred snakes no more than a hoot and a holler from the family doorstep.

The thick, dark woods held bears ready to attack and Indians to scalp. Homesteaders early learned to sometimes walk backwards rather than forwards. That way, an Indian up to no good, coming upon footprints on the forest floor, would be confused as to which way his intended victim might be going. Even in church every man had a rifle by his side while others outside stood guard.

With little knowledge of sanitation, no corner drugstore with remedies for infection, pre-natal care non-existent and even ill-prepared doctors scant, it is little wonder his boyhood was filled with superstitious sayings. Indeed, at any gathering, folk would more often than not share what they considered medical tidbits: steal a dishrag— kill a wart. Skip a row when you plant and there'll be a death in the family. Or, if a horse breathes on your child it'll get whooping cough. As late as 1859, if a doctor-to-be attended medical school at all, he had covered the entire store of existing medical lore in one year.

However, there was never a shortage of courageous dreamers who might die young but, as more than one would proclaim, "I'll die wilderness free." It wasn't that any self-reliant pioneer wanted complete loneliness. It was that he expressed a desire for more moving-around-in space by saying, "Don't mind a neighbor as long as he's not too close. But if I can stand at my front door and see smoke rising from his cabin, he's too close."

The question of slavery traveled with these new pioneers who were not men and women shy with their opinions nor reticent in their responses. One Lincoln historian has suggested that his lifetime dislike of slavery stemmed from having been, to a large degree, a slave to his father. Whenever there was any time not needed to work on their own property, his father would hire him out to a neighbor and keep the money for himself. Every muscle in Abe's body got a daily working over that might have killed some lesser men. He had no idea what lay beyond time's horizon, but he definitely knew he did not want it to be farming.

Because Abe was always more than persistent toward rightness, just before he finally left home he helped build one more family log cabin. It was finished four days after his twenty-first birthday, and then he left. God had work for him to do.

* * * * * * * * *

Chapter 2
The Making of the Man

* * * * * * * * *

Who was Lincoln, the man? We have had well over a century to try to answer that question and are still overwhelmed by the task for he fits into no convenient mold. When Lincoln was born, what did God have in mind? What did his Lord want him to be? All the hours he spent in church listening to sermons certainly had their influence. In all his decisions when he was president, he must have been guided by a Jesus who did not just look at the Via Dolorosa, but walked it. Who did not just partake of the Last Supper, but served it. Abe's Biblical learning must have underlined the thought that prayers must be more than just the turning of a prayer wheel. There is no record of his first heavenly appeal, but it is well established that he believed prayer is a conduit that can reach the heart of God.

Since he had no influential father and minimal formal

schooling, Lincoln could easily have adopted failure and given up. But if asked how he felt about fizzled success, he would have shared that it was but a ridge in the road on the way to fulfillment. He had no doubt that the only thing that held a man back was not wanting something badly enough and lack of preparation. "Give me six hours to chop down a tree and I will spend the first four sharpening the ax," he would often comment.

Abe's stretched-out-frame had spent many hours during the first two decades of his life clearing land and then plowing it. This, along with a good set of genes, gave him more strength than any other man in his county. No one could beat him in a wrestling match. Fact of the matter is he could sometimes put down two men at a time. One day, he actually picked up a 300 pound outhouse and carried it 50 yards. It took two men to carry it back to where it belonged.

God had given him a strong back, but he also wanted a strong mind.

Sometimes a father leads and his son follows. The path Tom Lincoln offered, that of a wandering carpenter, an illiterate dirt farmer and a guard for county prisoners, was not one Abe chose to walk. After leaving home he took on all kind of jobs: woodchopper and butcher boy, field hand and ferryman. He also became a tanner, a rail-splitter, a surveyor, a storekeeper and a postmaster. If variety is the spice of life, Abe's was hardly bland.

As it is for anyone new to the adult world, there were brief excursions into new experiences. It was a time of finding oneself, and Abe volunteered to fight in the Black Hawk Indian war. Fight is a misleading word. Though elected a captain, he saw no "live fighting Indians," but still lost a lot of blood to aggressive mosquitoes.

It was in New Orleans, while working on a flatboat traveling the Mississippi River, that he got his first taste of the slave trade in action. There, he saw human beings treated as inanimate property. It shriveled his soul as angrily he said, "If I get the opportunity, I'm going to hit it hard." His early upbringing had already cemented his decision that nothing about slavery was right. The small Mount Separate Baptist Church of his youth in Kentucky had preached against it, and Indiana, where he moved at about seven, was anti-slavery.

Whenever someone would comment that slavery wasn't so bad, he would reply that if it was so great the speaker should volunteer to be one.

Perhaps "honest Abe" is sometimes used with little thought as to the honesty of the phrase. Yes, he truly earned this label, for actually he was honest to a fault. He once walked three miles to return six and a quarter cents[1] to a woman he had mistakenly overcharged because of a faulty weight. The next day, having the same problem, store clerk Lincoln again walked miles to deliver a proper amount of tea to a customer.

Some of his friends told him that both were foolish things to do. His reply was instant. "I don't like thieves and I don't want to be one." Certainly what his Bible taught him didn't lessen this inclination.

Another time, a man had figured a way he could steal $600 legally. He just needed a lawyer to help him. It took no time at all for Lincoln to respond, "Oh, you're legally right, I won't argue with that, but you're morally wrong. Besides, you look like a right healthy young man. Why don't you go out and earn yourself $600 honestly?"

And honesty paid off. When he became a lawyer, people would ask Lincoln to represent them because they knew he could be trusted.

Later on in life when he was running for president, some-one wrote in a newspaper article that he read Plutarch. He had never read the philosopher and wasn't comfortable with the lie, so he borrowed a book by Plutarch and read it. Now when someone saw the article, it would be true.

He wasn't interested in being a liar, either. He used to say, "Lyin' don't stop trouble. It just postpones it. And besides, no man has a good enough memory to be a successful liar."

Could he grow angry like most men? The answer must be in the affirmative because he was human. Indeed, he wrote his share of exasperated responses. The difference is that having written them to settle down his dander, he would then throw them in the nearest stove. He was smart enough to be caustic, but also smart enough not to be.

Few could tell a joke or lay out a story with such ease and excellence as could Lincoln. Yet he never told stories that would be inappropriate in the presence of ladies. There was a special charisma and gentle thoughtfulness about him that put everyone at ease.

There seems to be aggressive agreement that he also never practiced profanity. It wasn't that there were no ample examples of cursing around him on a regular basis. It is just that early on he accepted the admonition not to take the Lord's name in vain and strictly held to it. He drank only once in his entire life, and then quickly decided that it was a great foolishness that only left him feeling "flabby and undone."

There was certainly nothing flabby or undone about his sensitivity. It was said he could not pass a fallen chickadee without putting it back in its nest. Once while riding, he stopped to rescue a pig stuck in the mud. The mud he acquired, as a result of the rescue, did not help his suit but it reinforced his compassion. This side of his personality showed yet another time when he gave his seat at a picnic table to an elderly woman and then quite happily finished his meal seated on the ground.

Was he then someone who spouted Scripture at every drop of an opportunity or wore a double-decker halo? Hardly. But if a scripture fit, he was not too shy to give it its place in the sun.

He loved riddles. One of his favorites was to ask, "If there were three ducks on a pond and one of them was to get shot, how many would be left?" Inevitably, someone would reply, "Two." "Ain't so," would chuckle Abe, "wouldn't be none left. The other two would fly away."

Oh, how he would later wish that the giant riddle which was

about to become a civil war would fly away. It was a conundrum too difficult to solve, so eventually everyone would stop trying and simply fight it out rather than think it through.

Prejudices against foreigners existed in the 19th century no less than in our own. But then, to be considered a proper American, one had not only to be native born but Protestant. Since Abe could not stand bigots, as he easily hearkened back to his own English roots, he would remind a repetitive hypocrite that unless they were an Indian it was hard to see how they could make a claim to be of native stock. To top off his comments he would often tell the story of the Irishman who, after being berated for not being born in America replied, "I would have, but my mama wouldn't let me."

His lack of prejudice extended to women, as well. In a time when the very thought was unheard of, he believed that they too should have the right to vote.

Quick wisdom and wit can sometimes be lifesavers. They certainly were one day when a disgruntled fellow attorney challenged him to a duel. Not wishing to shoot or be shot, Lincoln, who had the choice of weapons, suggested they do battle with "cow dung at five paces."[2] Heavy-hearted at having to give orders to kill, even during wartime, he might well have fought the Civil War this same way, if given half a chance.

Realizing that beneath his endless joking was a deep and fervent thinker, people were always asking him philosophical questions. Once a man asked, "What's wrong with the world, Abe?" "Same thing that's wrong with my two boys Tad and

Willie," he replied. "One day I only had three walnuts and each of them wanted two. That's what's wrong with the world. We live in a three walnut world and some would take all three if given half a chance, even all four if the number were expanded."

Everyone has played the old "What If?" game. And it is well worth the effort when it comes to Lincoln's final choice of a wife. His first love, Ann Rutledge, who died of typhoid fever at nineteen, was said to have the personality of an angel. However, Mary Todd, whom he did marry in 1842, was prissy-proud, arrogant and ambitious. But she cannot be quickly named and then dropped without further comment. The influence of a wife on a husband is far too great. And when that husband becomes the president of the United States, the influence definitely cannot be ignored. She firmly believed Lincoln would be a success. Even to envisioning him one day as president of this great nation and not shy in proclaiming it. Unfortunately, it can be said that she more often worked at making him famous than happy.

It was perhaps asking too much to expect her to really understand Abe's way of being. After all, he was a product of the wilderness and she was raised to be a lady and taught to speak fluent French. To say they were a mismatch from the start is an understatement, but it was not all bad. She did keep a nice home and was a good mother. The discipline she gave their children may have been too much, but the almost complete lack of discipline on Lincoln's part was certainly too little.

She also shared his abhorrence toward slavery. A close

relationship with her Negro seamstress Elizabeth helped her to develop this deep compassion for all "colored" people. These sentiments did not sit so well with her relatives in the South who were solidly behind the Confederacy. Two brothers and a brother-in-law fought and died for their beliefs.

While in the White House, Abe drove her crazy with old habits that died hard. Often when he wanted to read he found the floor more convenient than a chair. After all, that was how he had done it on the dirt floors of his boyhood. He never could get used to having servants either, and would more than occasionally answer the door himself. Abe simply was not one to put on airs. He must have chuckled whenever he thought of the Founding Fathers once considering calling George Washington *Your Elected High Highness*. He firmly believed that "Pride goeth before destruction, and a haughty spirit before a fall."[3]

Was there a complete lack of affection in their marriage? I think not, because it seems they did hold a mutual concern for each other. Their letters show that. And there were brief but poignant moments when actions also displayed it. When storms would cause her fright to the extreme, Abe would come home to give her comfort. When the worries of the war hung heavily, she would do all manner of comforting things for him. It was not that love did not exist between these two completely different individuals, it was just that her tumultuous temperament kept the waters constantly roiled.

Her on-going impatience did hone Abe's negotiation skills

that stood him well in later years. As if walking on eggshells, he would continually go out of his way to circumvent yet another of her temper tantrums. One example: when he wished to give $25 to a charity, he would quote $50 to Mary. She would promptly insist that was too much and cut the amount in half, which suited Lincoln fine since that was the amount he wanted to give anyway. He could have said $25 to begin with and spent the next hour arguing about it.

It may not have been a match made in heaven, but she did help him to more often recognize enemies than otherwise he might have. A constant victim of paranoia, distrust for her was a living thing. This emotional Achilles heel balanced the fact that Lincoln could be too trusting. It is, therefore, little wonder that this woman who, if someone was not an enemy, soon made them so. Mary was often like a little child awakened in a strange and unwelcoming room. What happened to her after Lincoln's death? She had long skirted insanity, and finally it came.

It must be added to these negative listings that for all their moments of turmoil, four boys were born of this marriage: Tad, Willie, Eddie and Robert. And Abe loved them so. Robert was the only one who lived into adulthood, but what if the other three had not died early on? Or what if theirs had been a childless marriage? Did the fact he had sons lean more heavily on his thoughts as he watched the sons of thousands of other mothers and fathers die upon the fields of battle?

He admitted to being greatly attracted to women, but despite so much home-delivered-chaos, he never broke his marriage vows. There was such a basic decency to the man. But what affect did a marriage that was, if not of hell at least of purgatory, have on the inner man? Would his presidency even have happened if he had married Ann instead of Mary? Suffice it to say, often men who do not find peace at home find success away from it.

I also find it interesting to speculate what Lincoln might have become if he had regularly attended a large academy in his quest for knowledge rather than sparsely attending a small one-room school. What if he had been born in a big house in the city rather than in a log cabin with one window and one door? How would the size of his upbringing affect the moral size of the man?

If raised in the lap of luxury, would the sense of privilege he would therefore carry give more or less peace either to him or the nation? Suppose his wealth had come from a Southern plantation. If surrounded by those who indulged his every whim would his thoughts and emotions have been that much different?

The rural churches planted proverbs that stuck with him throughout his life. One in particular, "Through the glorious telescope called faith I have viewed the worlds above." What proverbs would he have heard if his church of early choice had instead been a cathedral overwhelming some city corner?

Did the man we know develop in part from pushing a plow? Though he hated laboring in the field, could merely watching others engaged in manual labor ever be the same as doing it himself? And did poverty feed both his humility and ambition in a way no indulgent childhood ever could? He often said that God must have loved the common man because he made so many of them.

In seeking to define Lincoln, some have called him a genius, a benign incompetent, and others an idiot. He was neither, of course. But few, if any, who have truly studied his words and thoughts, would claim there was no strong under-girding of the spiritual. He was an exceptional individual who fit the particular needs of this country at a very troubling time. He once described his mind as being like a piece of steel. Very hard to scratch something onto it, and almost impossible afterwards to rub it off.

The character of a man can so often be seen in simple things. Even in later years when he had the choice of walking or riding in a carriage, he chose to put his loose-jointed frame to the enjoyable task of footing it. He felt it cleared the mind and inscribed more vigor to a day. It is interesting to note that this man, strong of mind, body and spirit, measured his decisions not on a scale of what was easy, but rather what was right.

★ ★ ★ ★ ★ ★ ★ ★ ★

Chapter 3
Early Politics

★ ★ ★ ★ ★ ★ ★ ★ ★

W hen this future president was only twenty-three and Andrew Jackson was president, Lincoln decided to become a candidate for the legislature in Illinois. His first political announcement did as much to explain the man as his platform: to improve the Sangamon River, change the usury laws and provide universal education. "Every man is said to have his peculiar ambition. Whether it be true or not, I can say that I have no other so great as that of being truly esteemed of my fellow men, by rendering myself worthy of their esteem. How far I shall succeed in gratifying this ambition is yet to be developed."[1]

His political philosophy, that government must do for the people what they sometimes could not or would not do for themselves, remained largely constant down through the years. Already in his young political life he had seen far too many who majored in observations and minored in performance. He felt strongly that an elected official should do something more than just bay at the moon.

He once suggested that many politicians and their campaign promises were like pants salesmen. "I've got pants for sale that are a perfect fit. Big enough to fit any man and small enough to fit any boy." Lincoln went on to concur that it didn't make any difference because they didn't keep their promises anyway.

Such traits, opinions and promises might have been enough to get him elected at his first try, but they weren't. But being eighth in a field of thirteen did teach him that the best of promises were no guarantee of victory. Neither was he comfortable being stuck in neutral, so failure for him was no more than a political hiccup. Believing that the secret to success is learning how to fail, he simply began again. His second try brought success, and four straight victories.

While Abe was not shy about his faith, neither did he believe that religion should be overly inserted in any campaign. By way of emphasizing this attitude, one day while debating with a preacher who was running against him, his opponent stood up in church and said, "Everyone who wants to go to heaven, please stand." Lincoln remained seated. The preacher continued, "Everyone who wants to go to hell, please stand." Lincoln again did not rise. "Just where are you going, Mr. Lincoln?" he was pointedly asked. "Me," he said with a sly grin on his face, "I'm goin' to congress."[2]

Early on he set a personal precedent of honesty that followed him throughout his campaigning. He had received $200 expense money at the beginning of an election try, and when he returned gave back $199.50. It had been given to him to pay for food and lodging but because his friends were many, his expenses were almost nil. For him there was no choice but to return all but fifty cents which he had spent on a barrel of cider at one of his rallies.

Just because he had lots of invitations to share a meal with friends didn't mean he always ate high on the hog. One time when served pigeon soup that was the worst he had ever endured, he simply ate it and kept quiet. Good manners and decent concern made him do this more than once in his travels. He did comment afterwards to another friend that he was sure they had not boiled a pigeon but rather the shadow of a pigeon that had starved to death.

Did he give thanks for the meal? Beforehand, probably. Afterwards, unlikely. Remember, this was honest Abe.

It required an unquenchable spirit to enter politics in this nation's early beginnings. Everyone was tough. They had to be for politics was a rough and ready art. There were those who would take anyone who heckled their candidate and literally throw him out into the street.

Again his rough and tough wilderness raising stood him well. At one of his meetings hooligans turned off all the gaslights and wouldn't allow anyone to turn them back on. Not easily daunted, he went on speaking as his people just continued to light matches.

Another time when he tried to speak, those for the opposition were less than willing to give him his chance. They stamped their feet, yelled, clanged cowbells and blew whistles. For thirty patient minutes he silently waited. When finally they wore out and gave up, he began his speech. He confided to a friend that he would have waited another thirty minutes if necessary.

You didn't even have to be a naturalized citizen to be able to vote for state offices in Illinois. In those years each state had its own way of doing things.

"This little engine that knew no rest…"[3] never read with an attorney, as did some. Abe was truly a self-made solicitor. His college of law was borrowed books. His classroom lit by a lamp of learning. Always a friend of dreams and goals, finally at the age of twenty-eight, he set up his first law practice in Springfield, Illinois.

Gregariousness came naturally to him and required no study or degrees. It was a good thing, because in his time lawyers traveled the circuit together, and their sleeping accommodations would be two to a bed and eight to a room.

The old stovepipe hats, so often seen in pictures of that era, were a foot high. This may seem to us a peculiar fashion statement, but actually they were mobile filing cabinets. Instead of modern day briefcases, lawyers and businessmen used their hats to carry letters, newspaper clippings, deeds, mortgages, checks and receipts.

It is also interesting how cases were often argued in newspapers as well as at court. Not press conferences or leaks, as is done today. Lawyers would actually pay for column space to present their side of an issue. Being a master of succinctness, Lincoln could usually say what needed to be said in only one column whereas other lawyers might need as many as six. Eventually, his Gettysburg Address would prove a prime example of such brevity and simplicity.

He loved to make light of his profession. It helped him keep a proper perspective. One of his favorite legal tales was of a man fined $10 for contempt of court. He gave the clerk $20 who promptly said, "I can't change this." "Don't make no matter," he replied. "This court deserves an extra $10 of contempt."

Always quick on his feet in a courtroom, he once entered an almanac as proof his client was innocent of a murder. "On the night in question, there was no moon. Therefore it was pitch black dark and he couldn't have seen to do it," is how he most likely put it.

His lawyering widened his acquaintanceships with the world. He handled everything from mercantile to manufacturing cases. He also learned that business can be perverse and overly greedy. Once, to finally receive $5000, his fee for representing a railroad company, he had to sue his own client. Honest Abe in a dishonest world.

He was still young in the profession when he spelled out his devotion for the law. In an 1838 Lyceum Address, he said,

"Let reverence for the laws be breathed by every American mother, to the lisping babe that prattles on her lap—let it be preached from the pulpit, proclaimed in legislative halls, and enforced in courts of justice. And in short, let it become the political religion of the nation…"

In notes for yet another lecture, he called on all lawyers to be peacemakers and good men. He argued that it ill befits any attorney to do nothing but stir up strife only so he can put money in his pocket. Catch 'em and cheat 'em was the way of some lawyers, and the world, full of lemmings, marched in lock step.

But not Abe. He always listened to whatever drummer he felt offered the best beats to follow. Then, with typical Lincoln attitude, proved he liked to practice what he preached. One day, having been asked for a legal opinion, he reached up on his shelf, brought down a book and read the answer. "How much do I owe you?" asked the man benefited. "Tain't nothin'," said Lincoln, "I should have known the answer without having to look it up."

He never had a quarrel with ambition or proper compensation. Just with greed. One year he actually made more than the governor of his state. Many people said he would never be a successful lawyer because he was too honest. They meant it as an insult. He took it as a compliment.

For ten of the seventeen years he lived in Springfield, Lincoln and his family worshipped in the family pew at the

First Presbyterian Church. When his son Eddie died, Abe, even though not a member, probably asked more theological questions than some who were members. But life goes on, and more than theological questions lay ahead. Places and events that would sear his soul far beyond anything he could ever imagine.

★ ★ ★ ★ ★ ★ ★ ★ ★

Chapter 4
Before the War Years

★ ★ ★ ★ ★ ★ ★ ★ ★

Calling a nation a *nation* does not make it one. A revolution had been fought to break away from England less than a century earlier. And although George Washington had refused a kingship, the South now felt it was all happening again. Some far away place telling it what it could, or could not do.

The war between the States was no new thought. For almost thirty years it had been simmering. In South Carolina, as early as 1832, medals were struck that read, *John C. Calhoun, First President of the Southern Confederacy.* In both North and South, abolitionists vowed to fight slavery until it became a distant miserable memory. In 1833, forty individuals formed the American Anti-Slavery Society and spelled out their stand. "We will rebuke slavery from every street corner. We shall put a printed tract in every hand. By political and moral persuasion we will bring slavery to its knees."

William Lloyd Garrison, publisher of the *Liberator* in Boston, Massachusetts, and co-founder of the Society, on replying to the complaint that he was too much on fire, simply suggested that it was necessary because he was surrounded by icebergs. Too often there was more than enough fire, on both sides, and not enough quenching to solve the matter.

Certainly Lincoln was aware of the undercurrents of distrust and alienation that were becoming as thick as ants on a pot of honey. In a town not far from where he lived, a Presbyterian minister bought a printing press and began to put out pamphlets against slavery. The local populace of Alton, Illinois took to this with about as much pleasure as putting stinkweed on the table and calling it a flower arrangement. "Stop!" they ordered. "Can't do that," was his reply. Thereupon, they threw his printing press into the same river that had delivered it from St. Louis. He simply ordered another one and went back to work. This time, in the middle of the night, they circled his warehouse and set it on fire. When he fled to escape the flames, they shot him dead.

Everyone wants freedom of speech, but many are not always willing to give it.

It did seem as if both sides had gone a little mad. And in looking for an answer to it all, the parable-making Lincoln said, "It's like my two boys Tad and Willie who were one day fightin' over a toy that each wanted. I said to Tad, 'Let Willie have the toy so he'll be quiet.' Tad answered, 'No sir, I can't. I need it to keep me quiet.'"

The entire mess was just as childish. Grown men forgetting to put aside their childish ways. Everyone wanting everything they wanted. No one willing to keep quiet.

The battle of words continued, and soon it would not be just pride but bodies that would suffer. Jesus talked to Christians on both sides, but they distorted His words of love and righteousness. Insults flew back and forth with an increasing crescendo. "It's not our fault, it's yours." "Is not." "Is, too." It all went from bad to worse as the final states joined the Confederacy. Men began to carry firearms, even in the hallowed halls of Congress.

Despite all the nation's troubles, things other than the possibility of war also captured the attention of the public. The popularity of the violent sport of prize fighting was on the rise. It was the mid 19th century, a time of such extravagant personalities as Edgar Allen Poe, Ralph Waldo Emerson, Herman Melville, and the great entertainment exploiter, P.T. Barnum.

A new invention, the Morse telegraph, allowed messages to reach their destination in a matter of minutes whereas a letter could take two weeks to be delivered. If speedy delivery could have resulted in speedy reasoning, the problems that brought on the conflict might have been resolved.

It was the time of Charles Darwin and more powerful microscopes. Even more powerful telescopes swept the dust of space.

Man was finding new worlds under his feet and above his head. Meanwhile he could find no peace or common sense.

Why? Because men do not often enough look for reasons and then do. Rather they do and then look for a reason for what they have already done.

A good example of such unreasonable thinking was the Mexican War (1846-1848). A war Lincoln spoke against while in the House of Representatives. "It's like the farmer who said, 'I'm not greedy. I only want any land that touches mine.'" It was acquisition needing a reason, and Abe wondered out loud as to whether it was legal, if the spot where American blood stained the ground was truly American ground.

It was a war that had followed the words of Frederick the Great, "Take possession first. Negotiate afterwards." Some argued that if we had not taken Texas we might have had to take it from the British, for England still had New World designs. Lincoln wasn't too sure we should try to take it from either.

He was not afraid to also suggest that it might well have been another attempt to extend slavery while cloaked in patriotism. It was an unpopular stand that put him at the risk of being called unpatriotic. That danger did not deter him. He was, as always, willing to pay the price of popularity rather than take the easy way and vote for what he thought was wrong. It was typical of Abe to paddle against the current.

It was not as if he had prepared for the future by taking up permanent residence in Washington. After all he was only a one-term congressman, from 1847 to 1849. But while there he soon learned about government waste. In those days the Army needed a steamboat to better fight the Indian wars in Florida.

The government, refusing to buy one for what they felt was an outrageous price of $10,000, chose to rent. When it was all over they had spent $100,000 for the rental.

Ole Abe did have a sense of humor, but he failed to laugh at this one.

The buildings of Washington were a beauty rising from streets that were a quagmire when it rained and a dust bowl when it didn't. He wasn't totally surprised to find that a stroll through town might pick up an accompanying pig or cow.

One congressman showed up for work in a blue, swallow-tailed coat, light cashmere pantaloons and a scarlet vest. He soon voted for improvements of things that didn't want to be fixed and wouldn't stay fixed even if the bill passed.

Lincoln wore basic black, and was fully at home with everyone no matter how they dressed because almost everyone was a lawyer. Whether they spoke with Yankee twangs or Southern drawls most were a quick-witted lot. One attorney, after he had received a Doctor of Laws degree from Harvard, was asked to say a few words in Latin. Since he didn't know any, he responded by harvesting a few words of Choctaw and then a little Cherokee. Since none of the listeners knew Latin either, it worked out quite well.

After his short sojourn in Washington, Lincoln actually retired from politics for five years. However, he simply could not long sit on the sidelines while the nation he loved grew increasingly ragged around the edges.

It was a fruitless task, his repetitive arguing that a divided Union could not long hold on to its unity. He knew that slavery, which was producing this boondoggle, had always been introduced without law and that law always came later as a way of legitimizing what was already taking place.

The whole process that was moving toward conflict took a giant leap when a novelist named Harriet Beecher Stowe exploded into the midst of the slavery controversy. Her book, *Uncle Tom's Cabin,* challenged the current thinking of 1852, and put dissolution on a fast track toward disaster. As the ideas in her unabridged commentary swept the country, Lincoln called her "the little lady who made the big war." It only proved what he had long known, that the written word could first capture a nation's attention and then the nation itself.

It may not be enough to use the word slavery and assume that everyone truly knows what slavery was really like. Since slaves were considered a commodity, there could be no argument as to the owners' rights to buy and sell them. And if this caused separation of husband and wife? No problem—at least for the owners. They were not considered married, only coupled. Their children? They belonged not to the parents, but to the master who owned them. Thought of, by some, as little more than animals, a cruel owner or overseer treated them as such. Lincoln often commented he could not be a master or a slave.

There were dangers in holding people in bondage. And so there were those who not only did not want to lessen the chains, they wanted to keep those ill equipped to complain even more enslaved by keeping them ignorant. Were there exceptions? Of course. Some owners would not practice cruelty. Even taught their slaves how to read and write, which, in the South, was a criminal offense punishable with jail time, or worse.

Did hypocrisy all this time sit on a kingly throne? Indeed. It always lives easily and well, even more so when profit is attached. Interestingly enough, slavery had long been held in such low esteem that those who sold slaves were ostracized. And while the plantation owner would allow his children to play with slave children, he would not let them play with slave sellers' children.

But true freedom? That was not so easily spread around. Even some blacks who were free now changed their minds as regarded freedom of other blacks and were ready to have a slave or two of their own. And there were Indians who had had their land stolen but now also dealt in stolen lives. Life for a slave was an arbitrary existence at best.

Lincoln could not buy into the idea that the slave in the South was better off than the hired hand in the North. In answer to such a supposition he simply pointed out that once he had been a hired hand and now could hire, and that it should be obvious to even the dullest that this was never true of the slave. He firmly believed that a society of equals was better than one ruled by aristocrats—that slavery and true equality could never co-exist.

Therefore, in a speech in Peoria in 1854, he sought to

explain his understanding of the South's position. "…I have no prejudice against the Southern people. They are just what we would be in their situation. If slavery did not now exist among them, they would not introduce it, if it did now exist among us, we should not instantly give it up. There are individuals on both sides who would not hold slaves under any circumstances; and others who would gladly introduce slavery anew, if it were out of existence."

While many argued that Lincoln wanted war, other opponents argued that he was living in a dream world when it came to his constant visions for peace. A dream that was becoming a nightmare, he must have thought. Our nation had mightily prospered beneath the wings of an enlightened Constitution. Why now choose guns? Why now choose bullets instead of brains?

By 1857, Lincoln was speaking out against the Dred Scott decision; a U.S. Supreme Court decision which basically said that the Declaration of Independence and the Constitution were for whites only. To say that it was a pro-slave decision would be an understatement. It was one more shovel full of dirt on the gravesite of freedom for all.

Without hesitation it stated that since a slave was property he had no right to sue for freedom, even though he was in free territory. Cleverly written, it claimed the sanction of the Constitution. It was simple and direct in arguing that slavery could not be outlawed in national lands because that would violate Southern property rights as guaranteed by the Fifth

Amendment. It raised a first class ruckus because many felt it was an open-door decision that would spread slavery everywhere in the United States. It certainly captured a firm place as one of the major causes of the Civil War.

It is unknown whether or not Abe used one of his own sayings to argue against the veracity of the decision, but if he did, he would have perhaps asked the question, "How many legs does a dog have if you call his tail a leg?" Then, answering his own question, "Still wouldn't be but four. Calling a tail a leg don't make it a leg."

Lincoln believed that the Missouri Compromise must be restored for the sake of the Union. "If it is not," he said, "the South, flush with triumph, will revel in excess. The North, feeling betrayed will seek revenge. One side will provoke. The other resent. The one will taunt. The other defy. Already many in the North and South willingly defy the Constitution when it does not suit their wishes."[1]

Meanwhile, some strange solutions were being proposed. One such outlandish suggestion was having two presidents: one from the South and one from the North. Let them alternate every four years. "Would this not be better than war?" asked some. Others, along with Lincoln, could see absolutely no reason to give a stamp of approval to division.

The words to an old song, "John Brown's body lies a-moldering in his grave..." may be about all some know of his disastrous raid on the federal arsenal at Harper's Ferry, his capture and his hanging. What John Brown did on October 16, 1859, cannot be condoned. What he said is worthy of consideration. "You say I am mad and I ask is it sane to keep four million human beings in bondage? Is it sane to think that slavery will always be?"

From London to Moscow, Prussia to Italy, rebellion was everywhere. People were weary of tyranny, and across the ocean in America lay escape—wide, open plains of rich black soil just waiting to be settled. The last thing the multitude of new immigrants wanted was to compete with slave labor. Yet slaves were still being smuggled into the country, as many as 10,000 a year.

And so those for the continuation of slavery cried out, "Go west, young slave owner." And those who had no slaves replied, "Not on your life. A free man, working alone, cannot compete with a plantation owner with slave labor. Or even a free man with one slave."

Impatience grew fat and irritable with the whole discussion. It is seldom a friend of peace. War clouds that had hovered on the horizon for years began to blot out any blue sky of hope. It was a morbid melody no one should have wanted to sing.

The air was ripe with radical change as the country moved from a republic to a democracy, giving the executive branch of government less and less power and the people more. America was still an infant, unsteady on its feet. Now two parents, North and South, were fighting tooth and nail to enforce their own beliefs.

As the threats of secession by some Southern states continued to grow louder, the voice of Stephen Douglas, Democratic Senator from Illinois, grew stronger and stronger. He believed that slavery was unsuitable for the territories and that if left alone it would never happen. Therefore, he was in favor of leaving it to the settlers of Kansas and Nebraska to decide for themselves. Lincoln was not willing to leave such a happening to chance. He saw that a nation "half slave and half free" would have to become two nations, whatever the cost. He could not just stand by and watch this take place.

In 1858, the seven Lincoln/Douglas debates, for the senatorial seat for the state of Illinois, took place. Lincoln did not win. However, they did thrust him into the national limelight and make his name more widely distributed as a possible candidate for the Republican presidential nomination.

The debates, sometimes three hours long, were inevitable because their disagreements on slavery's future were too strong to be ignored. It was hot, as always, beneath the summer sun, as they discussed the issues on which hung the survival of the Founding Father's dreams. At one meeting Douglas suggested that when Lincoln had spoken about a divided house, this was what he wanted. Lincoln paused, and with a sardonic grin replied, "No, there is a difference between expecting something and wishing for something. I expect to die. I am not wishing for it." He and logic were the best of friends.

These meetings were really more like celebrations. After all, politics was largely the only show in town. It was a way of "politicking" that makes today staid by comparison. Maidens dressed all in white with tri-colored scarves, brass bands blaring—at least one for each side, men, women and even children filling the air with their enthusiasm. Tar barrels burning, guns large and small discharging into the air, cannons roaring, the glare of bonfires, boys carrying rails to emphasize that this was once a rail-splitting man. Lincoln's rise from such lowly beginnings was a boost to the dreams of any child.

Standing on large, pine board platforms, Lincoln and Douglas were equals in their exercise of mind and tongue, but in their physical appearance they were in sharp contrast. Next to six-foot-four Lincoln, Douglas was almost a dwarf. A tiny gladiator who spoke with a stentorian voice. When it was Lincoln's turn to address the crowds, he stood with his hands clasped behind his back. And his voice, though not disagreeable, was quite high pitched and reached out to those at the very back. His manner seemed somewhat awkward, but he was never awkward in his thoughts and words.

It should make no difference how a person looks, but folk, in any century, size up what they see and often equate that with capabilities. Cartoonists and satirists had a field day with Lincoln's swarthy complexion, long arms, and gaunt body. "Gorilla," and worse, were used to describe him. But Abe's personality won out. There was always a great truthfulness in his manner as his gray piercing eyes searched the crowd in silence at each beginning. As if to give everyone time to prepare for what he was about to say.

One man leaving a debate reflected, "I felt so sorry for Lincoln while Douglas was speaking, and then I felt sorrier for Douglas when Lincoln made his reply." Another, after meeting him, called him a "delightful combination of fact and wisdom." Nathaniel Hawthorne described him as a man it seemed he had seen daily on a thousand village streets. This comment was made after their very first encounter.[2] He had the kind of charisma that made him an instant friend.

Some people went to any and all extremes to hear these men debate. One group traveled by what we today would call a travel trailer. It was a wagon pulled by thirty oxen, upon which stood a log cabin with a hickory tree actually growing by the door.

They even brought what must have been a family pet, for a raccoon could be seen residing in the tree.

Whether attending the debates in person or simply talking about what was being debated, a potbellied-stove-poll would have shown the majority did not want war. Be that as it may, there were thousands who had given up on peace. It was a slippery slope on which a relatively new nation could not find its footing. Recruitment on both sides increased, and so, the Civil War, not civil at all, would soon begin.

The old Whig party, of which Lincoln had been a part,

died and the new Republican Party surfaced in its place. Abe joined, became a state leader and worked to unify it against a Democratic Party that was in disarray. There is no doubt those debates thrust him out of backwater oblivion and into prominence. At the Republican Convention, "no Comanches, no panthers, ever struck a higher note or gave screams with more infernal intensity" than those gathered to make their position known. Out of this absolute bedlam would come a nominee for the highest office in the land. It came as a shock to the Seward camp that Abe won. Supposedly William H. Seward, who would one day sit on Lincoln's cabinet, had the nomination in the bag, tied with a knot beyond unraveling.

In no time at all, nine million in the South would shout a gigantic "No!" and secede. This division made Abe weep but it did not make him falter. He felt his divine calling too deeply. Lincoln would be successful in holding together his Party. He would not be able to do the same with the nation.

Chapter 5

The Presidential Election Years

Abraham Lincoln would be the first president not born in one of the original thirteen states, and it would not be an easy journey. Just getting nominated for the office had been difficult enough. It had taken three ballots before the Republican Party had a nominee. Against all odds, this fairly obscure man from the wilderness was placed on their ticket.

With his Presbyterian background, Lincoln might well have recalled that day in sixteenth century Scotland at the port of St. Andrews when John Knox fell to his knees on the dock and cried out, "God, give me Scotland or I die." That may well have been how Abe felt, "God, give me the Union or *it* will die."

All presidential candidates have their list of pet projects that propel them toward the seat of power. And their agenda often defines their presidency. A stubborn, aggressive chief executive, James K. Polk fought a two-year war with Mexico and as a result annexed Texas. William McKinley, a principled commander-in-chief, probably did not have global imperialism in mind when he began his years in office. However, he is best remembered for the brief Spanish-American War when the Philippines and other islands became U.S. dependencies. Besides preserving the Union, there were other accomplishments Lincoln early sought: a protective tariff, a national banking system, and federal aid for internal improvements including the railroad.

There is this thing about leadership that does not mean every idea has to be credited to the leader, but certainly there develops an understanding of what is accepted and even underlined. Therefore, it should come as no surprise that during his administration (1863) the words "In God we Trust" first appeared on our coins.

Nor does their influence stop with what they want to accomplish. Often it extends with equal vehemence to what they are against. An egotistical, yet selfless president, Andrew Jackson vetoed re-chartering a National Bank. Theodore Roosevelt saw businessmen building fiefdoms and with an unwillingness to see a kind of Middle Ages repeated, he went after them with unflagging vigor. In no time at all he had begun forty-four anti-trust proceedings.

And then, there are those candidates not elected who might have contributed to a significant change of events had they won. Our entry into World War I was much later than it probably would have been if flamboyant Teddy Roosevelt, in another try at the presidency, had not failed to unseat Woodrow Wilson. In 1940, the Republican Party candidate Wendell Willkie was a strong libertarian and a progressive advocate on race relations. Had he been elected, would there have been Civil Rights legislation sooner?

He also campaigned against the government's lack of military preparation for a war he felt would soon come. Would a better prepared nation have prevented Pearl Harbor?

National debts or surpluses. Wars fought or avoided. Civil rights gained or diluted. It is nothing new to call attention to how important is every vote. Indeed, anyone who studies history cannot ignore this obvious fact.

How much differently would government function if all elected officials were as good historians as politicians and statesmen? Too often leaders do not just re-invent the wheel, they also have to learn how to use it all over again. The school-of-yesterday is such a worthy teacher. It is a shame that so many who have shaped our nation's directions have not better studied and remembered the good and bad directions of the past.

Lincoln can be said to have been both a secular and a sacred historian. His love for such historical giants as Washington and Franklin are well known, and an oft repeated story tells how a maid, while dusting his office, would sometimes peek over his shoulder to see what he was reading. Often it would be the ancient writings of Job.

What difference did it make that Lincoln was elected? Consider that if Douglas had won, a middle ground of non-intervention would have taken place and slavery might well have moved west along with the pioneers. Since everyone at the time was dancing on the edge of a sword it is still not easy, even in retrospect, to reach a conclusion as to what might have been.

By the time of the 1860 elections, the nation's two party system was in shambles. Internal wars were splitting both Democrats and Republicans so that there was no longer just two separate, distinct points of view. Most mainstream Republicans, like their leader, were moderates and would say it was morality vs. immorality, economic opportunity vs. economic backwardness, hard work vs. a non-working aristocracy. But to radicals on both sides of the political fence "moderation" was a dirty word.

When the Democratic Party split, Stephen Douglas was nominated by the Northern Democrats. The Southern faction put John Breckinridge on their ticket. And a third party muddied the waters still further. The Constitutional Union Party picked John Bell as their candidate. When finally Abe won the election, it is doubtful he was surprised that he did not win by a landslide. Almost no one in the South voted for him. That bastion of political distemper had been a bottomless pit that nearly swallowed him up in defeat.

The final results for the entire country showed that actually only forty-two percent had given Lincoln their acclamation. The Electoral College system[1] saved the election for him.

It might even be said their 187 to 123 vote precipitated the Civil War. Destiny plays strange tricks in the lives of men and for a host of reasons, a winner, both hated and distrusted in the South as well as much of the rest of the country, now stood on top of a collapsing heap of dreams.

The nation had annexed Texas, negotiated a treaty with Great Britain for the Oregon Territory, and New Mexico and California had been added to the mix of thirty-three states. With a population of thirty million plus, this growing giant was suffering from growing pains and finding it difficult to survive. Not yet a century old, there was no real sense of unity.

Actually, the word united never had been a good and lasting fit. One big stumbling block to unity was the problem of states' rights vs. the federal government. All the important political decisions; education, health, public order, etc. had always been state functions, and the South simply did not want a federal government making decisions on when and where slavery could be practiced. Its feeling toward Washington was the same as the phrase found on countless covered wagons moving west, *The Eleventh Commandment: Mind Your Own Business.*

Lincoln's beard, as well as the thrust of the coming war, were both in full flow. He had begun to let his whiskers grow after receiving a note from a little girl in October of 1860. Grace Bedell, with childish enthusiasm, had shared in a letter to him the idea that his skinny face would look better with a beard. She was right when she wrote it, and even more so after he lost 30 pounds agonizing over the war.

Read the name "Lincoln" and it is not necessary to actually have a picture available. Like few others in history, his visage, with or without the beard, is engraved in the minds of almost everyone.

Over the years there had been half a dozen proposed constitutional amendments and four proposed congressional resolutions to try to appease everyone and save the Union. In December of 1860, seven days before Christmas and just two days before South Carolina became the first state to withdraw from the Union, the Crittenden Compromise was offered. A last-ditch-effort to placate the South and stave off the war, it proposed an amendment to the Constitution that would legalize slavery forever south of the Missouri line. This Compromise, with the backbone of a jellyfish, went on and on as to where slavery would be allowed and where not and under what set of circumstances. Simply said, if you were black and lived south of the line you were in trouble; north of the line, you lived where slavery was prohibited. It was playing Russian Roulette with a large part of humanity who had no control of the trigger. Compromise is sometimes a good and sometimes a dirty word. This compromise deserved no place in polite society.

Lincoln had been elected but not yet sworn into office and the Union was already coming apart. By the beginning of

February, six states had seceded; South Carolina, Mississippi, Florida, Alabama, Georgia and Louisiana. When South Carolina had passed the resolution to secede, one lawyer was asked if he would join the secessionists. He promptly replied, "Absolutely not. South Carolina is too small to be a republic and too large to be a lunatic asylum."

Four slave states did keep their sanity and did not secede: Delaware, Maryland, Kentucky and Missouri. If these last four had done so, it would have been disastrous for the Union. Missouri and Kentucky, as Confederate states, would have been the perfect positions from which to invade Illinois and Indiana.

A last futile attempt to dissuade the secession of other Southern states took place at a peace convention on February 4, 1861. Nothing came of it. Everyone claimed to want peace, but on their own terms. And so, four days later, February 8th, a monumental convention took place in Montgomery, Alabama, and the Confederacy gained official status. The next day Jefferson Davis was elected its first and only president.

This former U.S. Army officer and West Point Academy graduate had no idea he was in charge of an already sinking ship. His raging optimism would have been admirable if not proved to be so wrong. It is not that the Northern forces were better fighters but rather that there were so many of them. Nine million in the South and twenty-two million in the North made for a mathematical impossibility. With men such as General Robert E. Lee, whom Lincoln had first asked to lead the Union Army but been turned down, the miracle almost happened. This talented leader certainly did the best he could in a war he had hoped would never happen.

Many believed that if this was what the South wanted, let them have it. Others believed that such division could only bring disaster.

In reality, America was quickly becoming four countries: North, South, West and "Wait and See." Too few seemed to understand that once fragmentation began, it could all too easily become forever.

Meanwhile, James Buchanan was still president, and he majored in not understanding what the North-South misunderstanding was all about. Some confused on-lookers argued he was for secession while others argued he was against it. The truth of the matter is, he was neither a leader of the nation nor a voice for the South.

A decent question was being asked. Is this republic capable of defending itself? Europe came equipped with a ready response, "No, but a monarchy can. A monarchy is more stable."

Rumors bounced off other rumors. There was talk that Britain would recognize the Confederacy as a sovereign nation. Nothing would have been worse for the Union for then foreign alliances could have been created and thereby the possibility of foreign intervention. The only way to stop such a European induced disaster was to make the abolition of slavery a centerpiece reason for the war. Or at least of equal status with saving the Union. When it was finally underlined by the Emancipation Proclamation, the South was truly alone.

Anyone with an ounce of logic lodged in his brain knew that the outcome of the upcoming uncivil war would shape not just America but the world.

In Springfield, Illinois, a newly elected president made one request of his law partner, William Henry Herndon. Looking at the shingle on their office door that bore both their names, he asked that it stay exactly as it was, to await his return.

Many times as he prepared to move east to the center of this nation's government he wished out loud that he were more devout. It is certainly not that he wanted to be regarded as a saint, but he did state over and over again that without the assistance of the Divine Being he could not succeed. But with that assistance he could not fail.

Because there were so many stops along the way, it would take eleven days to reach Washington. "We're movin' so slowly," Lincoln said, "I don't think we'll get there before the resurrection."

Many were quite willing to see him permanently gone, not just to Washington but from this earth. Hate letters assailed on a regular basis. Finally a plot to assassinate him in Baltimore was uncovered, and by repeatedly reminding him, "You can hardly be a good president if you are a dead president," his friends were able to convince him to secretly depart Harrisburg. Accompanied by Alan Pinkerton and W. H. Laman in one lone car pulled by a single locomotive, no lights and telegraph lines cut, he came through Baltimore at 3:30 A.M. dressed in disguise. Many other lonely middle-of-the-night times lay ahead.

When word of his unorthodox arrival spread, so did the criticisms. That he dared to show wisdom to protect the presidency was mocked as cowardice.

Before he had ever taken the oath of office, the powerful *New York Herald* suggested Lincoln resign. He responded, "I will not repent for the crime of being elected. I will serve my term."

Indeed, once president, his attitude toward criticism never wavered. "If I were to read, much less answer, all the attacks made on me, this shop might as well be closed for any other business. I do the very best I know how, the very best I can, and I mean to keep doing so until the end. If the end brings me out all right, what is against me won't amount to anything. If the end brings me out wrong, all the angels in heaven swearing I was right won't make any difference."

By Lincoln's second term, the *Herald's* typesetting offered its readers a complete reversal of opinion. It no longer championed the South and slavery and actually was for his re-election.

Even from the heights of the presidency, Lincoln did not suffer from an overactive ego. He considered this great office far more important than he who held it. This wise humility allowed him to function at a higher level than would most during the Civil War. Or, as Jesus put it, "If any man desires to be first, the same shall be last of all, and servant of all."[2]

While many would have surrounded themselves with *yes*

men, Lincoln chose leaders who seemed best for the job, whether they agreed with his views or not. In some cases, he chose enemies for his War Cabinet. His Secretary of Treasury, Salmon P. Chase, was a radical while Lincoln was a moderate. Chase, who suffered from an overabundant ego, would continually threaten to resign, until finally Lincoln called his bluff and accepted the request. William H. Seward, his Secretary of State, was a conservative. It was an act of leadership genius and patience to keep these men so close at hand for neither were ever shy in expressing their opposing opinions. Lincoln, who was a listener, would quietly weigh their arguments and then firmly make his decisions. With typical wisdom he said it was infinitely better to hear first hand the thoughts of those who might otherwise disagree behind his back.

Stop slavery. Extend slavery. Make it illegal to help slaves escape. Let each state decide. The federal government must decide. There were Southerners who had come north to become abolitionists and Northerners who had gone south to become slave owners. It was all a house of mirrors, a series of contradicting solutions. Minds and morals got all mixed up as everyone just got madder and madder.

Every age comes up with what, at first hearing, seems unbelievable. While their number was limited, there actually were some Southerners who would willingly have taken segregation to the extreme. Re-instate the feudal system so that some whites as well as blacks could be enslaved. Their reasoning? A free society is unnatural, immoral and unchristian.

Lincoln did not believe that all men were equal in strength, intellect or talent. Such a conclusion would stretch logic until it broke. He did believe that all men were equal in their inalienable right to life, liberty and the pursuit of happiness. "We cannot give freedom to every creature on this earth, but neither must we impose slavery on others over whom we have control. Has more been given to you? That does not justify your taking from those who have less."

There was an almost Biblical quality to much of what he had to say. In seeking to give clarity to his words, this man of stories warned the nation to beware the wolf who cries liberty but means tyranny. "There was a shepherd who, coming upon a sheep with a wolf at his throat, drove the wolf away. The sheep, of course, was overjoyed and thanked the shepherd profusely. The wolf, however, was not happy at all. It was to be expected. The shepherd had given the sheep liberty from exploitation, but from the wolf he had taken away the right to exploit."

Unfortunately, he made his parable-point to a South that did not want to hear, so it fell on ears muffled by subjective opinions.

He grew so weary of the ceaseless talk of breaking a mighty nation into two separate entities. "If you pull out of the Union," he often asked his detractors, "where will you carry it so that you are no longer livin' next door to fellows like us? You're brave and gallant. You've proved that in other wars when we were one. But you are no better fighters than us than we are better fighters than you."

Truth was there for all to see, but in a war of redundancy it was the blind calling out to the blind, "Can't you see?" He would then sum up his feelings again, "If it comes to war, one side will win and both sides will lose."

When finally he had placed his hand on his beloved Bible and become the nation's 16th president, it can be said that his Address was a Lincoln masterpiece. There were bits of heaven scattered throughout these thoughts. Certainly Christ's commandment to forgive and keep on forgiving were strong in this inaugural moment. But the stuff of majesty was not enough. Truth is a shaky commodity and not easily recognized. "To those, however, who really love the Union, may I now speak... will...the ills you fly to (be)...greater than all the real ones you fly from.... Physically speaking, we cannot separate. A husband and wife may be divorced and go...beyond the reach of each other...but the different parts of our country cannot do this.... Can aliens make treaties easier than friends?"

He must have inwardly shook, not so much from the chill of that March day, but from the coldness of the attitude of a South that was offering a winter of discontent. He wanted no war. He called out for patience and peace. "My countrymen, one and all, think calmly and well upon this whole subject. Nothing valuable can be lost by taking time...Intelligence, patriotism, Christianity, and a firm reliance on Him who has never yet forsaken this favored land, are still competent to adjust in the best way all our present difficulty…I am loathe to close. We are not enemies, but friends. We must not be enemies. Though passion may have strained, it must not break our bonds of affection."

Still he had made it clear again exactly where he stood. That which the government has the government will protect. Then promising no invasion, he had given a prophecy and a warning to the South, "You can have no conflict without being yourself the aggressors."

A time line for destruction was set in motion and a new president had his work cut out for him. Lincoln could easily see that he might be the last president of the United States.

★ ★ ★ ★ ★ ★ ★ ★ ★

Chapter 6

THE WAR
The Beginning

★ ★ ★ ★ ★ ★ ★ ★ ★

To those who sought to blame Lincoln for the war, he simply stated that he did not seek it but neither would he be held hostage to peace at any price. "I was elected not to pursue my own delight but to uphold the Constitution."

He tried in every way he could to convince any who were pro-war that it was a giant mistake. He questioned what would happen if the South actually won such a war. And what of the Constitution? The South would no longer be under its protection. And slaves? With war, slaves would no longer be returned. Would they build a Great Wall of China letting no one out and no one in? Would not the consequences of conflict offer far more problems than solutions? Wouldn't everything be better for all citizenry if discussions continued as one nation rather than two?

His sermon for peace could find no one in the pew. He

only managed to solidify their animosity. A script for war was being written beneath a howl of emotions. It is to Lincoln's credit that four years later, when the war finally came to an end, he had managed to maintain his attitude of forgiveness. But then, he was only practicing who he was.

Logic sometimes wears strange garb. One gentleman pleading the South's cause said, "Secession is good. We will now be unified by division. Laws of trade will bind us together as they do with other lands. For we, now an independent South, can forget our hates."

However, a missionary who had served in China put out a warning that became no more than a wisp of smoke in an angry wind. "I have traveled the world and seen enough of what civil wars can do. I pray with every ounce of my being that we do not embrace such idiocy."

War is always about some men dying and other men talking. The Civil War was not dissimilar in this respect. Nor was prejudice reserved only for the blacks. The prejudice of one side against the other moved easily back and forth across the lines of mortal combat and political battle. North and South, each having no doubt who was right, made a miracle of peace next to impossible.

What caused the South to withdraw from the Union? Fear! Fear that their way of life would disappear. Fear that if slavery did not expand into the territories, it would cease to exist everywhere. Economic fear that they could not prosper, or even survive, without slaves. Fear of the loss of states' rights. Fear of change.

Their fear of new tomorrows was based on fact. The railroads were changing the South's strong influence in Washington by filling up the West with settlers who were not necessarily in tune with Southern thinking. Kansas, a free state, was called "Bleeding Kansas" because of all the little wars that took place, both by neighbor fighting neighbor and by raids across the border from Missouri, a slave state. The South, now a minority but refusing to accept the reality, acted as if it had a majority mandate, and was unwilling to recognize anyone who did not rubberstamp their demands. Lincoln called what they were trying to do a "Slave Power Conspiracy."

But even he conceded that one of their fears was real enough. As things were going, it looked as if down the road they would not be able to continue slavery. He had said flat out in his speeches before he was elected that the United States was a nation that could not continue half slave/half free.

And owning slaves was not just limited to those with plantations. In the South, one family in five had bought themselves one slave or more. Even the poorest white and freed slave yearned to have a piece of the slavery pie. Less Northerners feel too sanctimonious for having few slaves, it is worth remembering that this freedom-stealing way of life started out in both regions. It is just that in the North it proved unprofitable.

It can rightly be said that Lincoln wanted peace so badly

he was willing to trade a fort for a state. He offered to give up Fort Sumter if Virginia would stay in the Union. Briefly that State wavered, but in six days refused his offer and stepped into another country.

Finally, everyone was talked out and very tired, so weariness and war joined hands. On April 12, 1861, Fort Sumter awoke to the sounds of cannon fire. On a man-made island in Charleston Harbor, it was still under construction and now it was being de-constructed. For the Confederacy, it was more than brick and mortar. It was an irritating symbol of Northern dominance right at their doorstep, and men fight and die for symbols.

While still in Springfield, Lincoln had made the request that after his inauguration, "…either hold, or retake the forts, as the case may require."

It was not only Fort Sumter that was being besieged. Lincoln was also besieged by contradictory advice. Give up the Fort—show wisdom. Don't give up the Fort—show strength.

This praying man must have spent much time upon his knees seeking divine strength and wisdom. Ultimately, he simply directed that an attempt should be made to supply the soldiers with provisions only. If no Southern resistance was given, no force would be required. The Confederacy gave its answer and opened fire.

Nothing was simple. Early in the war there were Union men

in the border states of Missouri, Kentucky, Maryland and Delaware who still held slaves. It took a special blend of wisdom and patience to hold together such rampant contradictions.

Would the tragedies that come from all wars be even worse if some wars had not been fought? Yes. Tyrants seldom volunteer to give up their thrones or power. And political changes do sometimes require radical, incisive surgeries. So yes, some wars need to be fought.

Can it always be determined wisely whether a war is necessary or not? Not easily. Some generals, if given a chance to express their opinions, give them from the point of view of men who are in love with battle and see no other reason for their own being. And for some politicians, war can produce a guarantee they will remain in office.

Good things can come from war. Look at our Revolutionary War. We expelled England, at that time the home of one of the world's finest fighting forces. By so doing, we set a standard for a new kind of freedom that has been increasingly sought throughout the world.

By fighting the Civil War, we saved ourselves from having the Atlantic waves lapping on the shores of two separate nations. By the first war we birthed a nation, by the second we saved it.

Perhaps the best way to have destroyed the idea of war would have been to find an overwhelming, all consuming definition of peace. No such workable definition, however, has ever existed, only a great desire to win. A search for such an explanation brings up the old adage "all is fair in love and war" and but spells out the fact that there is sometimes little fairness in either. Therefore, both sides traded in their plowshares for sharpened swords. America, for all its beauty and freedom, never was completely an Eden. Now, it would become a jungle.

The North was ill prepared. There were only 17,000 soldiers ready to pay the price of dying for a cause that would eventually kill over 600,000 total on both sides. On April 15, 1861, Lincoln called for 75,000 volunteers to end the insurrection. The Navy was no better off, but the dye was cast and four days later a blockade of Southern ports was still put in place.

Soon after the fall of Fort Sumter, Lincoln had tried to sum up what was happening. "It presents to the whole family of man the question whether a constitutional republic, or a democracy—a government of the people, by the same people—can, or cannot, maintain its territorial integrity, against its own domestic foes."[1] There had to have been tears in his voice when he said it, for it did not take a prophet to see that it might all be lost.

How had Ben Franklin, whom Lincoln had read about in his childhood, felt about his nation's future? He could not know that in less than a century there would be a Civil War, but in 1787, after signing the Constitution, he threw it down upon a table and prophesied, "I'll give it 200 years." It was not that he did not believe in what this republic stood for. It was rather that he knew the greatest danger to freedom is freedom itself.

How Abe must have agonized that the time frame of the Franklin prophecy might be cut by more than half.

A few things the Founding Fathers did not specifically include in the Constitution and Bill of Rights. The Writ of Habeas Corpus was one of them. Led by these new thoughts on liberty, they must have deemed this freedom as elementary because the only mention of this writ relates to the powers of Congress and under what circumstances it can be taken away from judges.

It was not an easy decision for the new president to make. The first fifteen presidents never utilized this clause, but Lincoln felt he could not do otherwise. The war was pressing hard and many citizens in the Union were aiding and abetting the South.

The northern part of Virginia was packed with rebels. Mobs had attacked the 6th Massachusetts regiment in route to Baltimore. With the abundance of Confederate sympathizers ready to rise up with more riots and insurrections, it was a time for action, not a time for a balancing act. Without such strength of character Lincoln would lose more than respect. He might well lose control.

The Writ of Habeas Corpus was suspended in Pennsylvania, Maryland, and Delaware. It allowed anyone to be arrested without formal charges. Chief Justice Roger Taney declared that only Congress had the constitutional power for such an action. Lincoln did it anyway.

It led to 13,000 arbitrary arrests, and to some it seemed a suspension of the Constitution. A Maryland man was the first to feel the consequences of Lincoln's proclamation suspending this "writ of liberty." He had attempted to organize pro-Confederate forces and for this was summarily arrested by military troops and held prisoner. He appealed to a federal court in Baltimore for his release, which ordered him promptly freed. The officer at Fort McHenry said, "No."

Thereafter, anyone arrested for "insurrection" was subject to martial law. It was not a popular decision. But then, Lincoln was not trying to win a popularity contest. He was trying to preserve a Union.

Some in the North shouted, "Squeeze the South dry by blockading its ports and the River Mississippi." "Not enough. Fight a war and win it!" cried out others. Lincoln agreed with the latter statement. He had wanted no war, but now that it had come, he felt nothing would be gained by half measures and running from it.

Lincoln had long understood that if the South won it would revel in excess and if the North prevailed it would, feeling betrayed, seek revenge. He had seen it all with a terrible clarity, how both sides were willing to defy the Constitution when and if it suited their needs.

Three decades earlier William Henry Garrison, co-founder of the Anti-Slavery Society, had written that all slave contracts are "contracts with hell." Now they were coming due. No longer just a battle of words, soon there would be real battles fought and real blood shed. Some believed the war would last not much longer than a snowflake in the sun. The North might have more men but, the South argued, they had more patriotism. William Tecumseh Sherman warned that whatever fed the hungers of war it would be a hostility that could easily last four years or more. As if to underline his words, the first battle at Manassas, the Battle of Bull Run, painted a terrible picture of what to expect.

With blind, innocent optimism, Northern dignitaries and their lady-friends had gathered on hills just outside Washington, D.C. to watch the battle. They believed it would be an easy victory, but what followed was victory for the South and defeat for the idea of a short and almost bloodless war. Nearly 5000 men died there, more from the North than the South.

As the panicked onlookers fled before they became part of the battle itself, with them went the growing realization that in war there is no building, only destruction. Confusion in commands, rumors in abundance, and death by design. A bit of Hades come to call.

The North's defeat at Bull Run was the best thing that could have happened if the Union was to be preserved. It made the South over-confident and put the North in shock.

1861 was turning out to be a banner year for a beginning misery. An escalating series of terrible events would demand Lincoln pull up his own words of wisdom from the past to see him through what lay ahead. "You cannot escape the responsibility of tomorrow by evading it today." "Let us have faith that Right makes Might, and in that faith let us to the end dare to do our duty as we understand it."[2] "Die when I may, I want it said by those who knew me best that I always picked a thistle and planted a flower where I thought a flower would grow."

He certainly must have regretted a prophecy he made in 1855 for now it was coming true. "I think there is no peaceful extinction of slavery in prospect for us . . . the spirit which desired the peaceful extinction of slavery, has itself become extinct . . . . The problem is too great for me. May God in his mercy superintend the solution . . ."[3]

★ ★ ★ ★ ★ ★ ★ ★ ★

Chapter 7
THE WAR
The Middle Years

★ ★ ★ ★ ★ ★ ★ ★ ★

"It is said an Eastern monarch once charged his wise men to invent him a sentence, to be ever in view, and which should be true and appropriate in all times and situations. They presented him the words: *'And this, too, shall pass away.'* How much it expresses! How chastening in the hour of pride!—how consoling in the depths of affliction!"[1] Lincoln had quoted this story before the war, but now in the midst of all his frustrations he must have often wondered when "this, too, shall pass." Wondered as errors of judgment and inefficiencies combined and would not pass. Amazing blunders made by leaders disagreeing or seemingly unaware.

Totally frustrated with General McClellan, Lincoln finally replaced him with General Burnside. And then he moved on through a list of unremarkable generals. War is seldom the well-oiled machine some battle veterans would have us believe.

There was also inefficiency in recruitment. What thinking person would raise a recruitment shed almost side by side with a hospital receiving wounded? Yet in Boston this is what happened. Interestingly enough, pens continued to scratch out enlistments for more ninety-day wonders. There was a war to be fought and someone had to do it. Even these three-month enlistments paled in summer. After all, the needs of a far-off war could hardly overrun the needs of harvesttime. Finally, unpopular conscription that undermined the volunteer soldier would come. Eventually, over one million, off and on, would serve in the Federal Army.

Incredibly, few had envisioned all the maimed and wounded on both sides of the Mason-Dixon Line. Bullets would now proliferate because ballots had failed, until finally one day, like all wars, it would come to a final bitter end.

Every war is defined by victories and defeats. The well-known battles are the giant steps toward winning or losing. But to the common soldiers who slog through and too often die in all the no-name skirmishes, they are all a tearing of heart and soul.

It is why any identity of Lincoln has to be tied in with the Civil War, for he did not just know this intellectually, he felt it. It was here the depth and strength of his soul was tested. A lesser man would never have showed such spiritual stamina. It was not that he had not seen death before this time. The wilderness of his youth had shown how easily death and cruelty can become king. It is rather that as the endless battles, both large and small, won or lost, continued, he reminded himself that beneath it all lay fragmented hope.

As president throughout these harrowing years, he carried the twin burdens of adversity and power, all the while knowing that either could put a man down in a moment. He understood that he needed to remember with clarity and fortitude his own admonition: "Nearly all men can stand adversity, but if you want to test a man's character, give him power."

In early 1862, an ardent abolitionist Julia Ward Howe, who would one day become one of the leaders of the woman's suffrage movement, wrote a poem, "The Battle Hymn of the Republic."[2] Fighting men always need their marching songs, and her words, put to the tune of "John Brown's Body," became the anthem that motivated thousands of Northern soldiers on their way to kill or be killed. Its stirring message also reached Lincoln and became one of his favorites.

Unfortunately, it gave a glory to that which had too much gore and too little glory. And on both land and sea, the warring continued to rage.

March 9, 1862 birthed a new day in naval warfare. In the battle at Hampton Rhodes, Virginia, the mighty metal gladiators, the Monitor and the Merrimac, tried to sink each other with poor success. All day, the Confederate Batteries on Sewell's Point watched as this new class of fighting ship sought to do each other mortal damage.

It was the battle of a giant, the Confederate's ship, the Merrimac, against the Union's much smaller ironclad, the Monitor. The Merrimac was a monster in size, making maneuvering clumsy and requiring over twice as much depth of water as the Monitor. It also suffered from a troubled engine. The Monitor, a mere gnat in comparison, was faster, turned more easily and most importantly, had a revolving gun turret.

Though the Monitor won by default as the Merrimac steamed away, it really ended as a stalemate.

There was no stalemate in Lincoln's view of the war. Each day, as the conflict continued cold to the cry for peace, he must have considered a truth he had spoken more than once: "Without slavery, the rebellion could never have existed. Without slavery, it could not continue."

The shame of slavery in the nation's capital came to an end when Lincoln signed the District of Columbia Emancipation Act on April 16, 1862. Slave owners would receive compensation for the loss of their "property," approximately 3,100 newly freed slaves. Those slaves willing to colonize outside the United States were provided with up to $100 per person. This was an idea whose time had not come and not many took the government up on its offer. Altogether, the government paid out almost $1 million for the freedom of the District's slaves.

Lincoln, without consultation, had first put together his own larger Emancipation Proclamation. It made it evident that as rapidly as the Union troops advanced, the slaves would be made free. He called it an "act of justice." It was not the idea of his cabinet, and they therefore considered it no good.

As often happened in Lincoln's cabinet, there was much division on both the content of the broad Emancipation Proclamation and when it should be put before the people. Some had wanted stronger language in reference to arming of the blacks. Others had felt it was a poor political move and should be junked. Still others argued it would be ill timed if treated as a mandate while suffering defeats. It seemed foolish to peddle it into view in the midst of losing.

The more sensible view became the accepted one, that nothing be done until the North earned a suitable victory. Finally, a reluctant McClellan showed enough gumption to stop Lee's troops at Antietam. This half success (for he failed to pursue his advantage and follow Lee into Virginia) was sufficient enough to publish the Emancipation Proclamation.

In reality, it was a power-action that was neither legal nor binding. The federal government had not yet won the war and could hardly make the Confederacy obey its proclamation. Therefore, it could not actually deliver on what it promised, but the symbolism was there. And the world heard. As it received European approval, it also stymied any Confederate hope for recognition and assistance from them, in particular the United Kingdom.

It did lead 186,000 motivated Negroes in the North to sign up for soldiering when the number of white volunteers was shrinking. Without their help in the final days, the North might not have won. Certainly the war would have lasted longer.

And Lincoln? Having at last begun the process to place the mantel of freedom on four million slaves, he now felt more free.

Everything that happened in the war was not of blood and pain and hate. The best in man sometimes rises out of the worst. More than likely the story of what happened one cold day during the terrible battle of Fredricksburg reached Abe's ears and pleased the heart of this forgiving president. It was a dreadful battle that cried out for some miraculous act of empathy.

A Sergeant Richard Kirkland of Company E, Carolina Regiment, made a request of his commanding officer that was almost denied. He had looked too long at the tortured, twisted dead and dying men and could finally stand it no more. He sought startling permission to take water and aid to those dressed in both Blue and Gray.

"You may get a bullet in the back of your head, son," he was told. The soldier replied that he wanted to go anyway.

"May God protect you," said Major General J. B. Kershaw. A short time later, men on both sides of this field of agony and despair watched in awe as the young man vaulted over a bloodstained stone wall and walked unarmed and seemingly unafraid among the dead and dying. They saw him kneel down and cradle a fallen Union soldier in his arms, offer him a drink of water, rest his head on his knapsack and cover him with his own overcoat. And then he moved to another soldier nearby. This time it was a Confederate soldier.

Again and again throughout that long, pale December

afternoon, just eleven days before Christmas, Sergeant Kirkland returned with water until every living soldier, from both the North and the South, had felt his compassion and concern.

General Kershaw later wrote that not one shot was fired during that time. That never had he heard such silent respect. "No doubt," his pen etched, "all the trumpets of heaven resounded on this monumental day."

Things had not gone well for the North in 1862, so Lincoln breathed deeply and began to do what he did best—identify a problem and do something about it. It would have been far easier if he could have replaced General George McClellan, sooner better than later. In speaking of McClellen's strategy for victory, he said, "He has the slows." In fact, the Union had a whole parade of generals—Burnside, Hooker, and Meade—who proved to be better at parading than fighting. Second guessing is always easier, but nearly two years of doing too little, or not much more than nothing, was no way to win a war.

Much time and many lives would be wasted until Ulysses S. Grant came on the scene. Here was a general who would finally do what generals are supposed to do—fight to win. The prolonged battle for Vicksburg, Mississippi, would last four months and prove he had the mettle and the mind for victory.

There was an unusual ending to such a fiercely fought engagement. After the unconditional surrender at Vicksburg, both sides swarmed forward to give congratulations for each other's courage. There was no gloating by the victor. Northern doctors ministered to Southern wounds. It was as if now that they no longer had to outdo each other in battle, so they sought to outdo each other in courtesy. It was the kind of behavior Lincoln gloried in.[3]

Working in unity with subordinates William T. Sherman, George H. Thomas and Philip Sheridan, Grant would coordinate a large scale battle plan for winning the war that became more than just Lincoln's concepted dream. It would become a reality.

Everyone was not gung ho for the war. Therefore, when patriotism on either side waned, drafting became a necessity. In the South they began to take men as young as sixteen and as old as fifty-five. The North soon followed suit. In New York City the measure was met with violence.

It seems to be an unwritten law for some that when there is disagreement do not debate, rather riot. However, there was a plan behind the madness. Lists of those to be drafted were destroyed and the building that housed them burned. Unfortunately, city streets became battlefields and innocents became victims. Thousands practiced violence to avoid having to go to war to practice violence.

In searching for the man, it is always necessary to read what was written about Lincoln in his own time, as much or more than what is written of him now. In this mid-time of the

Civil War, when there was so much animosity aimed in his direction, he still received articles of appreciation. *The Buffalo Express* newspaper spoke of his "remarkable moderation and freedom from passionate bitterness." They then added what should be a part of any discussion about this man, "We do not believe that Washington himself was less indifferent to the exercise of power for power's sake."

The Liverpool (England) *Express* called him a "lanky American" and wrote, "no leader in a great contest ever stood so little chance of being the subject of hero worship as Abraham Lincoln." However, this newspaper concluded that his inner qualities—his faithfulness, honesty, resolution, insight, humor, and courage—would "go a long way to make up a hero."

It can be said there was a war within a war. In his own Republican Party divisions multiplied and personalities clashed. Where the war should go and how to get there—radicals and conservatives fighting like coons and cougars.

He mused more than once that his sense of humor helped him to keep his sanity during the carnage. Such as one day when he asked a man if he would take his coat into town. A question returned, "How you gonna get it back?" "Simple," replied Lincoln, "I'm going to be wearin' it."

In July of 1863 he invited the people of the United States to invoke the influence of the Holy Spirit to help and guide the government to greater adequacy. The Union was at stake. It was not long after this, in October of the same year, that ole Abe established an official Day of Thanksgiving. He declared it "fit and proper that the gifts of God should be solemnly, reverently and gratefully acknowledged."

Everyone remembers Lincoln's Gettysburg Address, given on November 19, 1863. Too often the mortality of so many men, marching and dying with such precision, gets lost in the majesty of his message. It had been a three-day-long engagement that had to be fought, and that was the shame of it. Men advancing into the largest battle fought in the Civil War with flags bravely fluttering, as if on parade, all because politicians on both sides had paraded ideas that none would patiently consider. So, many would no longer be husbands or fathers, sons or brothers. Now silent, unable to listen to the dedication of their National Soldiers Cemetery, with the 15,000 gathered where they had fought. They had earned the right to lay there. It was a right many would gladly have given up.

Edward Everett, who had also run as Vice President to Senator Bell on the Constitutional Union Party ticket in their attempt to defeat Lincoln, was the primary orator of his time. That day, he spoke for two hours. His verbosity was reported but not half so well remembered as the President's pithy paragraphs.

While many considered Lincoln's speech too short and simple, Everett afterwards wrote, "I should be glad if I could flatter myself that I came as near to the central idea of this occasion in two hours as you did in ten minutes."

And so Lincoln, who had been invited only as an after-thought, gave his short, simple and heartfelt speech, forever after called the Gettysburg Address:

"Four score and seven years ago our fathers brought forth upon this continent a new nation, conceived in liberty, and dedicated to the proposition that all men are created equal.

"Now we are engaged in a great civil war, testing whether that nation, or any nation so conceived and so dedicated, can long endure. We are met on a great battle-field of that war. We have come to dedicate a portion of that field, as a final resting place for those who here gave their lives that that nation might live. It is altogether fitting and proper that we should do this.

"But, in a larger sense, we cannot dedicate—we cannot consecrate—we cannot hallow—this ground. The brave men, living and dead, who struggled here have consecrated it, far above our poor power to add or detract. The world will little note, nor long remember what we say here, but it can never forget what they did here. It is for us the living, rather, to be dedicated here to the unfinished work which they who fought here have thus far so nobly advanced. It is rather for us to be here dedicated to the great task remaining before us—that from these honored dead we take increased devotion to that cause for which they gave the last full measure of devotion—that we here highly resolve that these dead shall not have died in vain—that this nation, under God, shall have a new birth of freedom—and that the government of the people, by the people, for the people, shall not perish from the earth."

It would not all be in vain. The Union would be preserved. Unborn millions would live in a united rather than fragmented society. What is both sad and uplifting is to realize that without the war Lincoln would not have made the mark on history that he did.

Over and over again during his presidency Lincoln had tried to put into proper words how difficult, but eternally necessary, it was to hold the United States of America together as one nation. The Gettysburg Address put it better than he ever had before. It is interesting to note that one of the changes he made in his speech, as he spoke, were the words "under God." While some accounts vary, without exception, all reporters noted his reference to the Almighty.

It would take the politicians and military leaders longer than the common man to know that, for all intent and purpose, the war was over. While courage caused many on both sides to continue to fight, many others began to drift away to find what was left of the lives they had had before.

It is not to say that desertion is ever good. It feeds anarchy. It is to say that leaders need to more quickly realize that when the writing is clearly on the wall, it is time to put away their personal ambitions and settle the affairs of war as quickly as possible.

Lincoln believed that arrogance and over-zealous ambition warped the spirit. "We should be too big to take offense and too noble to give it." And, "I have been driven many times to my knees by the overwhelming conviction that I had nowhere to go. My own wisdom, and that of all about me, seemed insufficient for the day."[4] "When I am getting ready to reason with a man, I spend one-third of my time thinking about myself and what I am going to say and two-thirds about him and what he is going to say."

In the middle of a war an arrogant president would have been an invitation to disaster.

★ ★ ★ ★ ★ ★ ★ ★ ★

Chapter 8

THE WAR
The Last Years

★ ★ ★ ★ ★ ★ ★ ★ ★

Abe's hair, despite all his worries, stayed largely black. He liked to tell people overly worried about their growing gray hairs to leave them alone. "Pull out one and seven more will come to the funeral," he would say and then laugh uproariously.

Besides employing laughter to see him through, in a private letter written in September of 1864, he shared, "I am much indebted to the good Christian people of the country for their constant prayers and consolations…"[1]

It was in this same month that a group of African-Americans gave him a Bible. As he accepted it, he said, "In regard to this Great Book, I have but to say, it is the best gift God has given to man. All the good Saviour gave to the world was communicated through this book. But for it we could not know right from wrong. All things most desirable for man's welfare, here and hereafter, are to be found portrayed in it."

There are many accounts told of this man about whom it was said that he was slow to smite and swift to spare. In fact, during the war the generals pleaded with him to leave military discipline to the military. One of the classic cases concerns a deserter about whom he wrote, "Must I shoot a simple minded boy who deserts, and not touch a hair of a wily agitator who induces him to desert?" There were 331 such pardons.

He was not so kind to slave traders, refusing to pardon a man who "could go to Africa and rob (a mother) of her children, and then sell them into interminable bondage....(He is) worse than the most depraved murderer." "If slavery is not wrong," he wrote in 1864, "nothing is wrong."[2]

Lincoln visited the wounded more than once. He could not do otherwise to these men swarmed with pain. Such carnage was the natural outgrowth of steel and anger thrust toward those who otherwise could just as easily have been friends. The only gladness he could find in that hell was the touch of heaven brought down by the courage and compassion of countless women. In the heat of the day or at night by the dimness of lanterns, they walked among the horror, and to the best of their ability tried to make it less so.

This is but a portion of one of many letters Lincoln personally wrote to parents whose boys would no longer be coming home.

"Dear Madam,

I have been shown...that you are the mother of five

sons who have died gloriously on the field of battle. I feel how weak and fruitless must be any words of mine which should attempt to beguile you from the grief of a loss so overwhelming.... I pray that our Heavenly Father may assuage the anguish of your bereavement...

> Yours, very sincerely and respectfully,
> Abraham Lincoln."[3]

It was late summer in 1864 when Sherman's army captured Atlanta. Ten weeks later, from this jumping off point, 60,000 men began a march through the heart of Georgia to the ocean. Destruction of everything in between was the goal. Homes and almost every other standing building were sacked with appalling efficiency until what had once been beautiful was utterly destroyed and forlorn. Delivered by some men who did so with regret and by others who had lost their last vestige of kindness.

It was Sherman following his own instructions, "...modern wars are not won simply by defeating armies, but by destroying the ability to wage war—wreck railroads, burn fields, eradicate all economic resources—war is not glory—war is hell—and every man, woman and child must learn the lesson quickly."

The swath of devastation was sixty miles wide and three hundred miles long. Tons of provisions, destined for Lee's army, were seized. Trains were marooned in trackless wilderness, and vast gaps of emptiness took over where bridges had stood. This display of military mightiness was supposed to frighten the dove of peace into a flutter of life. It only made the South more resolute.

In Washington there was nothing Lincoln could do when things in the field got out of hand. He was their Commander-in-Chief, but he could not be everywhere. He could speak with an unrelenting concern, but his words could not control every soldier dressed in blue. He watched and prayed that the weariness of war, if not wisdom, would make it all soon come to an end. And when that finally happened, that good men in both North and South would outnumber the bad.

The army reached Savannah three days before Christmas. Some called it an early Christmas present for the nation. It was ill advised to use this description in conjunction with a time set aside to celebrate the birth of the Prince of Peace.

The march ripped the South to shambles all the way into the Carolinas.

During those critical times, President Lincoln and Dr. Phineas Gurley, pastor of the New York Avenue Presbyterian Church, had an agreement. A little used door to the church would be left unlocked so he could slip in unnoticed. Seated in a darkened room next to the pastor's study, with a door slightly ajar, he listened to the Thursday night Bible study.

One evening, two young men in attendance noticed the partly open door and the shadows of two men. They thought no more of it until it happened again the next week. Two men sitting in the same position in the darkened room, one with his head tilted as if listening intently. After the service they dashed outside and around to the door. They were too late to see the men but found footprints in the snow. One set was extremely large. The White House was not that far away and they arrived just in time to see the President slipping inside.

Confronting Dr. Gurley, he confirmed their suppositions and swore them to secrecy. It wasn't until after Lincoln's assassination that the story was revealed.[4]

These were not the actions of a man who went to church only to make a good political impression. This was the conduct of a seeker searching ever deeper into a truth he had already been speaking of so often and so well.

As the elections of 1864 approached, there had been movement within the Republican Party to oust Lincoln. His comment had been, "It is not best to swap horses while crossing the river."[5] He was fighting for national unity and could not even find it within his own party. A kind of truce developed and he remained his party's candidate.

General George B. McClellan ran against him as a Democrat. He lost.

On February 3, 1865, Abe met with Confederate Commissioners on a steamship in Hampton Rhodes, Virginia. For peace to progress, he demanded that reunion be a part of any peace arrangement. He was far more comfortable with trying to make a peace than he had ever been in having to fight a war. Fort Sumter was fading into the past. Appomattox gleamed on a not far away tomorrow. Even the most pessimistic could see the war was coming to an end.

There once was a war that lasted one hundred years. That would have been hard for anyone in those days of destruction to imagine for only four years had devastated people, places and things beyond belief. There should be little doubt that come evening time beneath the shifting light of a gas lamp, President Lincoln often looked for solace in the Bible. His "best gift of God" was always close at hand.

The day was cloudy, but as Lincoln stood to give his Second Inaugural Address on March 4, 1865, the sun flooded through. It made Lincoln's "heart jump." He was speaking to a nation now crisscrossed with scars and the agony of it spilled forth as his words reached out. "Both parties deprecated war; but one of them would *make* war rather than let the nation survive; and the other would *accept* war rather than let it perish....Fondly do we hope—fervently do we pray—that this mighty scourge of war may speedily pass away.... As God gives us to see the right, let us strive on to finish the work we are in; to bind up the nations wounds. . . ."

A reporter for the *London Spectator* described his words as "the noblest political document known to history."

Lincoln worried right up until his last day about the new

problems peace would bring. Plantations were in ruins. Slaves, with no skills or promises of employment, would be asked to make a living. The Emancipation Proclamation had been proclaimed but still held no legal status. Limbo for four million non-citizens was a real possibility.

The Thirteenth Amendment abolishing slavery would still be a hard fought victory—a large number of whites were fighting to maintain the Union rather than rid the South of slavery. Lincoln did not want to prolong the war but neither did he want it to be a monument to four wasted years with no positive conclusions.

It was all a recipe for disaster, but after four years of being miles apart, generals Robert E. Lee and Ulysses S. Grant finally met at Appomattox Court House. Southern boys in the Army of Northern Virginia waited nearby with their horses, which could easily have been taken as spoils of war. Grant chose otherwise. Word of his decision sped quickly down the line. "You boys take your horses on back home with you. You'll be needing them at planting time."

At the same time Lincoln was preparing to finalize what for him had become a personal need and planting time—to make a public profession of faith on Easter Sunday, 1865, at the New York Avenue Presbyterian Church in Washington, D.C. It is a fitting tribute to his honesty that he had waited so long to join a church. It would have been so much easier for him if had just joined earlier to stop the sniping of his critics.

Did this profession of faith, that never happened, have the

blessing of a pastor for whom the words "Christ and him cru-
cified" came often? It did, indeed. The grandson of Dr. Gurley
underlined this fact when he said, "My grandfather was very
conservative in his beliefs and would never have said he
(Lincoln) was ready for church membership unless he
believed sufficiently and had real faith in Christ."

But it was not to be. Pastor Gurley, who had so often pri-
vately prayed with Lincoln at the White House, now sat all
through the night with his friend and president and watched
him die. [6]

★ ★ ★ ★ ★ ★ ★ ★ ★

Chapter 9

After the War

★ ★ ★ ★ ★ ★ ★ ★ ★

I f Mary Lincoln had not instigated another of her famous feuds it might never have happened, at least at this time in this way. She had raised the ire of the wife of Ulysses S. Grant and so Julia Grant refused to attend the play at Ford's Theatre in her company. Had the General been present that evening there might have been more guards. Instead, the Lincolns sat alone enjoying "Our American Cousin," until John Wilkes Booth put a bullet in his head. It placed him in a coma and pushed the nation further toward chaos. The time was 10:15.

The next morning at 7:22, April 15, 1865, not long after his 56th birthday, with his second term of office only forty-one days old, Abraham Lincoln died. He, who did not want to impale the South on the North's sword of victory or practice revenge, was victim of both. His death from a misguided sense of duty could hardly have been a greater mistake.

As his breathing came to an end, it is said that Edwin Stanton, his Secretary of War, commented, "Now he belongs to the ages." Peace that he had not known for quite some time finally came.

After it happened, lawlessness wore a general's hat and was in complete control. Washington, D.C. was engulfed in riots, no longer the place of safety that it had been no more than fifteen years earlier when President Zachary Taylor had walked the streets alone, unguarded and unafraid. A soldier shot a man for saying of the assassination, "It served him right." Vice President Andrew Johnson was now president and his plate was full.

John Wilkes Booth, son of a distinguished theatrical family, had taken on all kind of roles on the gas-lit stages. Once he had portrayed the dismal Hamlet. Now he would play out another tragedy, convinced his deed would change the South. In an avalanche of twisted thinking, his real life drama took the President's life and would be the most counter-productive thing he had ever done. He was right about the change. He was wrong about the conclusion.

Much has been made of the fact that Lincoln's death took place on Good Friday, and that while Christ died for the world, Lincoln died for his country. Certainly he was no saint, but he was a good and kindly man who brought his Christian heart to Washington along with his head.

He had continued to speak out for the bigger picture right up through his last public speech on April 11, 1865. He had known that the winning of the war was but the first chapter of the greater manuscript called winning the peace. Obviously, others only knew that they did not like what they perceived he was thinking. The macabre solution? Dislike the thinking, destroy the thinker.

There is something about this martyr that captures the imagination. While physically he towered above his contemporaries, there was also a towering inner strength that had allowed him, when Appomattox was not even a day old, to reach out with forgiveness. He had made it clear he could not agree with what the President of the Confederacy had done, but understood that Jefferson Davis had pursued what he thought was right. That was reason enough for Abe to offer healing rather than hate. With equal fervor neither did he aim any malice toward General Robert E Lee.

Lincoln had seen a house of cards about to fall and realized how it could establish a precedent that would truly destroy what the Founding Fathers had created. Divided by two, in short time it might well have become a division of three. The Northeast, once not sure if it even wanted to be part of the original thirteen colonies, might then have pulled out. A few years down the road, some state in the Confederacy, unhappy with the new uniting, might have done the same. Bad habits come easily and are slow to leave.

It had been written all during the war that Lincoln was special. In 1861 he had said, "We must not be enemies. The mystic chords of memory stretching from every battle-field, and patriot grave. . . will yet swell the chorus of the Union."[1] In his final days he simply proved it.

It is not to say he had a crystal ball, but like many others he had known that a divided America could too easily be picked over by a restless Europe. There was a good possibility that Spain, France and England would have returned and given it all a second try. In the case of England, a third attempt, for with bitter optimism they had fought on our shores again in the War of 1812.

The Confederacy, this government of eleven states, had almost brought down a nation. It never had more than 750,000 troops, nowhere near the size of the Northern fighting force. To move troops and supplies, their 9,000 miles of railroad tracks were certainly inadequate to the task. The North had two and one half times that. They printed money, but with blocked ports and shrinking exports it soon had little worth, until finally it was nearly worthless. They were courageous, but courage by itself, against overwhelming odds, is almost always bound to fail.

Now that the war was over there was no shortage of solutions. Many conservative Democrats and Republicans simply wanted to revert back to the status quo with slavery still a viable option. Rebuild the plantations, even reinstate slavery. Such thinking failed to realize that slavery was more than a bad habit that needed to stay around because it would be too difficult to break. It made little sense to have sacrificed over 600,000 lives and end up with the old Southern ruling class in power, but it was seriously proposed. It was just as seriously rejected.

The magic word was reconstruction. Some called it a new chance for Negroes in a South that needed a rebirthing. Some called it a redemption period. Others said that it wouldn't work because proper repentance must come before redemption. Reality described it as a series of complications wrapped in a multitude of challenges.

Lincoln had been for a "general amnesty." Thousands, hearing these words, laughed in his face. And these few shining words of hope were soon eclipsed by the continuing dark and troubled presence of prejudice. All the issued statements in the world could not make everything fit and proper overnight. "Humpty Dumpty" had taken too great a fall.

It is a wonder things turned out as well as they did. It was obvious some miracles needed to take place. The Confederate States' infrastructures were totally destroyed. The economy was in shambles. Schools and churches lay empty or demolished. Black and white poverty was rampant. The work force and style of living could never be the same. The entire concept of reconstruction would lose much of the enthusiasm that had been present in its beginning. In only a dozen years, the number of radical Republicans trying to advance the rights of

African-Americans would be greatly depleted. Personal political opportunities became more important.

The kingdom called Cotton might be devastated, but Southern Democrats would not just sit silently on the sidelines. They once had power and they were gaining it again. Emotions, as tattered and patched as the clothing both black and white wore, raged and ruled the land. And so, what should have been done then would have to wait almost a century before a Civil Rights Movement could gain some muscle and respect.

The North had cried "treason," the South "freedom." Both sides translating their cries to read "truth." Lincoln had argued not only for maintaining the Union but also that "…in giving freedom to the slave, we assure freedom to the free."[2]

It is little wonder that once the war was over, wretched memories fed anger loud and long. Neither side could be proud of some things that happened during the war or at their many prison camps. The meanness in some men had multiplied. They felt their uniforms allowed it.

Andersonville, or Camp Sumter as it was officially known, in southwest Georgia is remembered as one of the worst. By the end of the war, it had held 50,000 prisoners on a piece of land no larger than twenty-six acres. Some men had called pits in the ground their home. During its short fourteen-month existence, 13,000 soldiers who had survived in battle died in captivity under the most terrible conditions. When the war was over the superintendent was hanged.

Camp Douglas in Chicago was often referred to as the North's Andersonville.

There, one in five prisoners died. In one four-month period, 1,091 starved or froze to death in the devastatingly cold winter of 1864. Because of lost and/or ill kept records, it is not known how many Southern soldiers actually died there, but a monument reads: "Erected to the memory of six thousand Southern soldiers here buried who died in camp Douglas Prison 1862-5."

The obstacles were monumental. It was a time that called out for great acts of responsibility by both whites and Negroes. Some rose to the challenge. Most did not. John R. Lynch, out of slavery no more than six years, was elected to the Mississippi Legislature at age 22. He continued to rise above his beginnings by becoming Speaker of the State's House of Representatives, served three terms in Congress, and spent a lifetime challenging the racial and social order of the south and the nation. Tunis Campbell, an African Methodist Episcopal minister from New Jersey, set up an independent colony for blacks on Georgia's many sea islands. Marshall Twitchell, a veteran of the Fourth Vermont Infantry, U.S. Colored Troops, fought for the rights of former slaves in Louisiana. Frances Butler, the daughter of a Georgia rice baron, driven by what was right rather than greed, negotiated a contract with her former slaves.

Why did so many others do nothing and were nothing? Most likely simply because it was the easier road to follow.

Was Lincoln, before he died, overly proud that he had so much to do with the preserving of the Union? It is more likely that he quoted once again words of one of his favorite poets, William Knox, "Oh, why should the spirit of mortal be proud?" As he walked the streets of Richmond, Virginia, in an unannounced visit after that city had fallen to the North, it was said that he was the man of the people among the people. When an elderly Negro had run toward him shouting praise, Lincoln lifted his hat and bowed, and wiped away a tear or two.

To his credit, the President had never been willing to settle for anything less than "this nation under God" and an acceptance of the challenge for a new birth of freedom. He firmly believed that once the war was ended it would be time for the fatherhood of God and the brotherhood of man to combine and make a healing. How good it would have been if the nation could have united behind a Lincoln who never wanted anything but peaceful negotiations. The assassination proved it was more easily said than done.

Lincoln had been wise enough to realize that "no exclusive, and inflexible plan" could "safely be prescribed."[3] The whole post war condition was one of shifting sand. All Southern states could not be treated the same because they were not all the same in record or response.

But even if he had lived, it would have been one political battle after another. Many in the North did not want to give kindness and many in the South were not ready to receive it.

While it made sense to slowly allow normality to return by

the reforming of state governments, the majority in the North demanded military occupation, the confiscation of estates, and political power as well as land transferred to former slaves. They were more than willing to cut down even the tiniest tendrils of hope for the Southern white population. They believed totally that the victor deserves the spoils.

Among the whites in the South, rebels were in the majority. Those willing to give re-union a chance were few and those willing to vocalize such disloyalty to the Confederacy even more scant. The war-storm clouds had scattered but peace, surrender or not, was not in complete control.

If Lincoln had not died he would have given the South back its pride as soon as possible. Some may refuse to accept the Lincoln his words portrayed. Others may find it difficult to see so much of a Pollyanna future, had his life been spared. Yet, even the most negative should be willing to admit that more charity and less malice could have begun to save some of the day. This leader had so often spoken as much like a philosopher/theologian as a politician. Not haranguing the South for its foolishness or suggesting punishment, but rather advocating too much forgiveness that never sat well with what was still a divided house. The death of many of his dreams followed his death. Hatred of the South was an easier sell.

The nation needed another president who could believe as Lincoln had, that it was time to "bind up our wounds." Instead they got Andrew Johnson.

EPILOGUE

The Thirteenth Amendment, outlawing slavery, was finally ratified by the States on December 6, 1865, leaving the Emancipation Proclamation in its shadow. Lincoln did not live long enough to see this happen. He was long dead by then, but his eyes had seen the glory. The Great Emancipator had done his job as best he could.

It was not easily passed—the first time rejected by the House. But in 1864 and 1865, by the use of Lincoln's power of persuasion and the help of some Democrats, it had gained its two-thirds vote and become a reality. Lincoln could have waited for the newly elected House to be convened with its Republican majority, but he felt the time was now. And when he felt something needed immediacy, he gave his all to get it done. It is well he came to the conclusion not to wait. He had little time left for such a luxury.

A prime endorsement for the President, as well as the deed, came from a former slave, Frederick Douglas, who gained much respect among both blacks and whites. He said of him, "In all my interviews with Mr. Lincoln I was impressed with his entire freedom from prejudice against the colored race."

The Constitution was finally no longer color blind. It would have been a far better reality if the same could be said of the many whites who still were. The Ku Klux Klan and voting rights restrictions soon appeared after the Civil War, as well as anything and everything that could keep the schism alive and well. Emotions ruled the land. Officially slavery was past and a new society awaited any black willing to grab the brass ring. Unofficially the Union Army could offer no safety guarantees.

Lincoln would have worked harder at making things right. His successor, President Andrew Johnson, seemed dedicated to keeping things wrong. Many have called him the worst possible president. His appointments as governors of Southern states were pro-slavery. The new governments promptly began to effect legislation to turn the clock back and freeze the calendar. To be a black after the war was to wed frustration and constant peril. An ex-slave could be arrested and fined for the crime of not having a job. Then to help pay off the fine they would be hired at ridiculously low wages. Buy land? Even if somehow enough money could be saved, the laws prevented a former slave from purchasing property.

They were called black codes and they were as dark as their name. No work or travel without a permit. Separate legal systems. It was 1865, and Jim Crow laws were already in place. Every single public building had separate facilities.

William Lloyd Garrison, in a burst of optimism and perhaps also fatigue called for disorganizing the Anti-Slavery Society. Black activist, 47-year-old Frederick Douglas, pointed out such action was premature. "Slavery is not abolished until the black man has the ballot."

It is interesting to note that the Negroes had a friend in the Republicans, if not for the right reasons, still a friend. They were afraid that as Southern Democrats gained more and more power, they would have less and less. It was obviously to their advantage to push for Negro rights.

No mending of so much unraveling would be easy. All these men and women with a background of being told what to do must now become masters of the art of decision. Slavery might well have a new name but by any name it still was slavery.

There was a Civil Rights Act, vetoed by Johnson, but passed in 1866 anyway. Unfortunately, it flew about as easily in the South as a lead balloon.

It was still the divided nation that Lincoln had feared, but America was in one piece, even if ragged beyond belief. And many, now realizing what they had almost lost, no longer called themselves by the name of their states. Rather than saying, "I am a Virginian...I am a Pennsylvanian..." the phrase became, "I am an American."

The United States has endured to celebrate its bicentennial anniversary and move into a third century of democratic survival. The memory of Lincoln has survived equally as well. There should be little doubt his belief-driven attitudes, words and actions were monumental in their impact, even after his assassination.

There will always be those who continue to ignore his faith-fed comments as if they never existed. It is enough to counter that he spoke too often and too well of God for the fact to be ignored.

V. Neil Wyrick as Abraham Lincoln.

Neil Wyrick's unique, original scripted One Man Drama of Abe Lincoln includes a question and answer session in which he opens the floor to questions not just about Lincoln's 19th century, but the 21st century in which he finds himself. For scheduling at your church, conference, college or convention, call 1-305-665-8686 or visit www.speakerneil.com for more information. You may wish to order a video of the monologue portion of this performance from Camco Productions. It is actually a film shot at a 150 year-old home and interspersed with many old Civil War photos. Visit the Camco web site www.camcoproductions.com and then click on "Abe Lincoln."

V. Neil Wyrick's illustration of Abraham Lincoln.

NOTES

In some cases Lincoln's words are paraphrased, time and place unknown.

Preface

1   "It is the duty of all nations..." Proclamation of a day for National prayer and humiliation, signed by Lincoln on March 30, 1863.

2   "With malice toward none..." 2nd Inaugural Address - a theological as well as political statement.

3   "I invite the people...." A national Proclamation of Thanksgiving, July 15, 1863.

4   actual quote "...I cannot explain it, but soon sweet comfort crept into my soul..." July 5, 1863.

5   "It is the duty of all nations..." Thanksgiving Proclamation on October 3, 1789.

6   "Statesmen may plan and speculate..." 1787 Constitutional Convention.

7   refers to the book of Micah 4:3.

8   February 21, 1861 Address to New Jersey General Assembly.

9   "My concern is not whether..." A comment he made more than once in answer to a question about God's will.

Chapter 1 In the Beginning

1   "As a man thinketh..." Proverbs 23:7 (KJV).

2   "Wisdom is the principal...." Proverbs 4:7 (KJV).

Chapter 2 The Making of the Man

1   The quarter cent was borrowed from Spanish currency and was still in use in Lincoln's time.

2   "The Humorous Lincoln" by Keith Jennison. Other references to the same duel speak of broadswords but still show that Lincoln was not inclined to give bodily harm. When James Shields, the attorney who had challenged him refused to negotiate peace, Lincoln with his long arms simply struck off a small branch above him thus proving it could just as easily have been his head. Attorney Shields now willingly called off the duel.

3   "Pride goeth before destruction..." Proverbs 16:18 (KJV).

Chapter 3 Early Politics

1   "Every man is said..." First political announcement, New Salem, Illinois, March 9, 1832.

2   debate with Rev. Peter Cartwright, evangelist, 1846.

3   statement about Lincoln by William Herndon, Lincoln's law partner.

Chapter 4 Before the War Years

1   "If it is not..." Lincoln's response to the Missouri Compromise on Oct 16, 1854 in Peoria, Illinois.

2   Insights and descriptions of Lincoln gathered from "The Hidden Lincoln," from the letters and papers of William H. Herndon, edited by Emanuel Hertz, NY, 1938.

Chapter 5 The Presidential Election Years

1   Each state sends a number of delegates to the Electoral College equal to its number of senators and representatives in Congress.

2   "If any man desires to be first..." Mark 9:35 (KJV)

Chapter 6 The War— The Beginning

1   "It presents to the whole family of man..." Lincoln's War speech to the Senate and House of Representatives, July 4, 1861.

2   "Let us have faith. . ." In an address in New York City.

3   " ... I think there is no peaceful extinction of slavery ..." Letter to George Robertson, Kentucky lawyer and professor, August 15, 1855.

Chapter 7 The War—The Middle Years

1   "It is said an Eastern monarch. . . " Address before the Wisconsin State Agricultural Society, September 30, 1859.

2   THE BATTLE HYMN OF THE REPUBLIC

Mine eyes have seen the glory of the coming of the Lord;
> He is trampling out the vintage where the grapes of wrath are
> stored;
He hath loosed the fateful lightning of His terrible swift sword;
> His truth is marching on.
I have seen Him in the watch-fires of a hundred circling camps;
> They have builded Him an altar in the evening dews and damps;
> I can read His righteous sentence by the dim and flaring lamps:
> His day is marching on.
I have read a fiery gospel writ in burnished rows of steel;
> "As ye deal with my condemners, so with you my grace shall deal;
> Let the Hero, born of woman, crush the serpent with his heel,
> Since God is marching on."
He has sounded forth the trumpet that shall never call retreat;
> He is sifting out the hearts of men before His judgment seat:
> Oh, be swift, my soul, to answer Him; be jubilant, my feet!
> Our God is marching on.
In the beauty of the lilies Christ was born across the sea,

With a glory in his bosom that transfigures you and me;
As he died to make men holy, let us die to make men free!
While God is marching on.

3   "Port Hudson: Its History from an Interior Point of View" by Lt. Howard C. Wright, St. Francisville Democrat, LA, 1937, reprint ed.; Baton Rouge, The Eagle Press, 1978.

4   ". . . I have been driven many times . . ." From a conversation with a friend, Noah Brooks.

Chapter 8 The War—The Last Years

1   "I am much indebted..." Letter to Eliza Gurney dated September 4, 1864.

2   "If slavery is wrong..." Letter to Albert Hodges dated April 4, 1864.

3   "I have been shown . . ." Letter to Mrs. Lydia Bixby dated November 21, 1864.

4   Lincoln and Dr. Phineas Gurley, American Tract Society—a non-profit organization, Publishers of Christian literature since 1825, Oradell, New Jersey.

5   "It is not best to swap horses..." Reply to National Union League, June 9, 1864.

6   The source of this information is a grandson of Dr. Phineas Gurley, Dr. Melville Gurley. From a magazine article, "Lincoln Went to Prayer Meeting," by Leslie Flynn, *Christian Life*, February 1949.

Chapter 9 After the War

1   "The mystic chords..." Lincoln's First Inaugural Address, March 4, 1861.

2   "In giving freedom to the slave..." Second annual Message to Congress, December 1862.

3   "no exclusive, and inflexible plan..." From Lincoln's last public speech, April 11, 1865.

BIBLIOGRAPHY

50 Great Americans
by Henry Thomas & Dana Lee Thomas
Doubleday & Company
Garden City, NY, 1942

Abraham Lincoln
by Carl Sandburg
Charles Scribner's Sons
New York, 1950

Abraham Lincoln, His Path to the Presidency
The Review of Reviews Corporation
New York, 1929

Lincoln Special in Life Magazine
February, 1991

On This Day in America
by John Wagman
Gallery Books
112 Madison Avenue
New York City, NY, 1990

One Night Stands with American History
by Richard Shenkman & Kurt Reiger
published by William Morrow and Company, Inc.
New York, 1982

R. E. Lee
a biography by Douglas Southall
Charles Scribner's Sons
New York, 1935-36

The Heritage of America
edited by Henry Steel Commager & Allan Nevins
Little Brown & Company
Boston, 1951

The Hidden Lincoln
By Emanuel Hertz
Viking Press
New York, 1938

The Humorous Mr. Lincoln
By Keith W. Jennison
University of Illinois
Urbana, 1953

Lincoln: Speeches and Writings, 1859-1865
The Library of America
New York, 1989

The March of Democracy
by James Trunslow Adams
Charles Scribner's Sons
New York, 1932-1933

The New Encyclopaedia Britannica
15th edition, Helen Hemmingway Benton, Publisher
1974

The Story of America in Pictures
arranged by Alan C. Collins
Introduction by Claude G. Bowers
The Literary Guild
New York, 1935

The United States Experiment in Democracy
by Avery Craven & Walter Johnson
Ginn & Company
New York, 1947